"*Vic Johnson's tried and true invigorate your imagination a life you dream.*"

~ Jim Rohn, America's Foremost Business Philospher

"*One chapter into the book and already I have made a 'dream list.' I am looking forward to doing the other 12 action steps in the book. I find that when an author has you take action steps, you're no longer just reading a book, you are taking a class. A course if you will.*"

~ Amazon reader review

"*Vic's writing style has a way of taking timeless wisdom and putting it in words that are down-to-earth and easy to understand.*"

~ Amazon reader review

"*This book contains no 'fluff'. Vic Johnson brings information together from many sources and he tells it like it is. Each chapter has action steps to reinforce the ideas as you learn them.*»

~ Amazon reader review

"*Very well worth reading. Having run my own business the last few years that has seen its share of successes as well as failures I can relate to many of the things written in this book and look forward to putting into practice the advice given.*"

~ Apple iBookstore reader review

GOAL SETTING:

13

SECRETS OF WORLD CLASS ACHIEVERS

Vic Johnson

No Dream Too Big Publishing

Melrose FL

GOAL SETTING:
13 SECRETS OF WORLD CLASS ACHIEVERS
Vic Johnson

Get a FREE Smart Goals Worksheet and Video
http://www.Get-Smart-Goals.com

Published by:

No Dream Too Big Publishing

No Dream Too Big LLC

PO Box 1220

Melrose, FL 32666 USA

www.Goals2Go.com

Book design by Sue Balcer of JustYourType.biz

ISBN-13: 978-0-9838415-7-9

Table of Contents

Preface

WE LIVE IN A TIME where many people have lost touch with the qualities that produce extraordinary lives. Imagination, ingenuity, drive, and a no-fear, no-quitters allowed mentality often seem to be disappearing from our culture and our world.

Fortunately, that's only half the story. More and more people are learning just what they are capable of achieving. Ordinary people are learning how to achieve extraordinary things! This is a book for everyone who has ever had a dream. This book will teach you how to set goals and achieve that dream, step-by-step and day-by-day.

You'll discover some great news! If you've been struggling, if you've ever felt like you were going "nowhere fast," you'll learn that it's not because there's something intrinsically wrong with *you*. You'll learn, instead, that it has a lot to do with ways of thinking that you've adopted in the past. This is *great* news because you can change the way you think, speak, and act.

Success isn't the result of winning some sort of lottery. It's the result of applying the right principles with the right action and the right mindset.

Do you feel like you're stuck? Do you feel like you've been watching life pass you by? Then this book is written with you in mind.

Adopting a victim mentality, blaming outside circumstances, and retreating back to your comfort zone are easy. Deciding that "nothing will ever work" is also easy. But with that attitude you will continue to be stuck with the results you've always had. If you're truly ready for different results then you need to be ready to do something different. Or as the popular expression says, "if you always do what you've always done, you're always going to get what you've always gotten."

This is a "doing" book. You won't get much benefit from this book if you just read it cover to cover. You'll find exercises at the end of each chapter. The information in the chapter presents principles—the exercises get you started on the "how." Doing the exercises also gets you into the habit of taking action on the information you have learned.

Taking action is vital. Many people read many personal development books, yet never manage to make a change. Reading the book fools them into thinking they are doing something, but nothing really happens.

So take the exercises seriously if you want to get the most benefit out of this book! You'll see the results quicker than you think. So let's get started…

Why this Book Matters to You

My name is Vic Johnson. You may know of me from one of the many personal development websites I've developed since 2001. At AsAManThinketh.net we've given away over 400,000 copies of James Allen's little classic. At MyDailyInsights.com we provide a daily message of hope and inspiration to 100,000 subscribers every day. At Goals2Go.com and our Champions Club, we've provided goal setting programs, software and other solutions to thousands of people around the world for more than ten years. And there are more sites, but I won't bore you with all the details. I think you get the picture that we've got more than a little bit of experience in helping people achieve what they want.

You may know me from my best-selling book, *Day by Day with James Allen*, which is five-gold star rated at Amazon.com. Or from my appearance along with Jim Rohn, Brian Tracy and Denis Waitley on the Jim Rohn Weekend Leadership Event DVDs, the biggest event of Jim's illustrious career. Or from my TV show Goals 2 Go on the TSTN network.

Finally, if you're one of my old creditors, you may know me from the days, not that long ago, when my family and I were evicted from our home and later lost the last automobile we had. Those are days I'd just as soon forget, but all of the lessons learned during that period have shaped who I am today and make the information you're about to receive much more valuable. I assure you that I don't intend to offer you any college textbook theory. This is life-changing and, for some people, even life-saving material.

I must warn you in advance. I've never been accused of being diplomatic. Sometimes my delivery is right between the eyes, and sometimes you're probably not going to like (or agree with) what I've got to say. But as they say down here in the South, "the proof is in the puddin'." The proof IS in my puddin' and the puddin' of all the World-Class Achievers presented here. Learn to like our puddin' and your life is about to get very interesting.

WHY I DECIDED TO RELEASE 13 SECRETS

Since 2001 we've produced goal setting products for our subscribers. From low-priced basic self-study programs to full-blown coaching and consulting solutions, we've helped thousands of people the world over to reach new levels of achievement.

In every year since, I've had the same recurring set of questions about goal setting. This year, instead of answering the emails and phone calls I thought I'd share some of the inside "secrets" of what I've learned from some real World-Class Achievers. These are people I've studied, been mentored and coached by, as well as those I've coached and mentored myself in our Champions Club.

To be blunt about it, I'm more than a little ticked off by a lot of the misinformation about goal setting that's been passed off by people who couldn't achieve a goal if their life depended on it. Even though this "cheap" book is giving away valuable information that others have paid significant amounts of money to learn, at least I'll know the truth is getting out there instead of a bunch of hokum.

"For so many years I set goals, only to see them remain incomplete…"

But the biggest reason I'm sharing the 13 Secrets is because of the letters I frequently receive like this one from Hollywood musician John West of Beverly Hills: "For SO many years I set goals, only to see them remain incomplete and transferred from one year to the next. Sometimes I might actually see a goal achieved, maybe two, but there was never any structure to these successes and there was little hope the succeeding year would be any different." (This is just part of his letter—more coming later).

I've heard it from thousands of people besides John, and I've experienced the frustration myself. This book is my contribution to helping you understand that the same secrets used by the World-Class are available to you – and they're there for the asking – just waiting for you to receive them.

So, make sure your seat back and tray table are in the upright and locked position, buckle your seat belt and get ready to learn **13 Secrets of World-Class Achievers.**

(Attention All Eagle Eyes: We've had a number of people proof this book before we released it to you, but there is a chance you might spot something that was missed. If you find a typo or other obvious error please send it to us. And if you're the first one to report it, we'll send you a free gift! Send to: **corrections@vicjohnson.com .)**

Secret #1:
Big Doers Are Big Dreamers

MARCUS AURELIUS, who rose to become Emperor of the Roman Empire, shares one of the most important secrets of World-Class Achievers: **"Dream big dreams; only big dreams have the power to move men's souls."**

Procrastination is one of the biggest complaints I hear from the people we work with. And generally speaking, I believe one of the two main causes of procrastination is a dream that's too small (the other cause is *belief*, which I'll cover later). It's just too easy to put off doing something that doesn't have a lot of appeal even if you were to achieve it.

Big dreams drive us to do things we'd never do for lesser dreams—in many ways they almost pull us through the obstacles we're likely to have on the way to reaching them.

Having a specific meaning and purpose in your life helps to encourage you towards living a fulfilling and inspired life.

Animals cannot select their goals. Their goals of self-preservation and procreation are preset. There is no changing that fact, at least not in the short-term. Animals' success mechanism is limited to instincts, preset goal images.

Humans, on the other hand, have something that animals don't have.

Creative imagination.

Not only are humans creatures, they are *creators*. We can

formulate a variety of goals. We can go after whatever goals we choose! We actively control our creative mechanism by choosing what we want to achieve.

Our creative mechanism works automatically, endlessly, 24/7, to achieve whatever goals we tell it to achieve. If we don't consciously choose our goals, our creative mechanism still works, but usually on negative goals. Goals of failure, goals of success, they make no difference to our subconscious. Turning your creative mechanism from a failure mechanism to a success mechanism is a very simple process.

Stop presenting your internal software with negative goals and images, and just replace them with success-centered goals and images! Your self-image has a DIRECT EFFECT on your results in life. It will continue to operate as it always has, repeating past results and outcomes, UNTIL you take ACTIVE control over it.

It's not a social convention or a result of culture that causes us to make goals for ourselves. We're hard-wired for it! Our prefrontal cortex, the front 1/3 and most evolved part of our brain, is hardwired to help us generate and achieve goals. Being goal-oriented helps us to keep our behaviors on track and use our brain to its utmost ability.

In Denis Waitley's book *The Psychology of Winning*, he states that there are three types of people involved in the game of life:

First, there are the spectators. These are the majority of people. They act as bystanders, watching life happen around them. They avoid trying anything new or desirable for fear of being hurt, defeated, ridiculed, or rejected. They spend their lives watching life happen on television. They take a passive rather than active role. Most of all, these spectators fear winning. Winning brings the burden of responsibility, for being a good role model, and setting a good example. Rather than make the little necessary effort to change their life for the better, and play a more active role in their destiny, they sit back and watch others achieve their dreams. They watch television so that someone else can do their thinking for them. They use television as a way to escape from their own thoughts. Brian Tracy would agree, for he said, "people who have no goals are doomed forever to work for people who do."

Next are the losers. They prefer to be like or act like someone else. They spend their time criticizing and nitpicking others. Losers are easily spotted because they quickly and readily put themselves and others down.

Finally, there are the winners. They are the few who seem to effortlessly acquire what they want from life. They set and accomplish goals that help not only themselves, but also other people.

It is your personal responsibility, and yours alone, to actively invest the time, study, and effort needed to learn as much about your brain, self-image, and self-talk as possible. Doing so will put you above the rest of the people that remain passive in regards to their life. They allow life to just happen to them. By studying these principles, these "secrets," you will gain control over your thoughts, over your goals, and ultimately over your life!

Living a life of big dreams is a lot easier than you might think. It's really just a decision. Here's a great lesson from the World's #1 Goal Achiever:

When he was just 15, John Goddard was inspired to

create a list of 127 "life goals" (he called it "My Life List"). On a simple, yellow legal pad the young boy listed things he had fantasized about. Many of the experiences he dreamed of he had first encountered reading the encyclopedia (he grew up without television and read the encyclopedia for entertainment).

When I met John for the first time, the young seventy-something told me that he has accomplished 111 of his original 127 goals—PLUS 500 others he set along the way!

Here's just a few of the ones he's reached:

- He's climbed many of the world's major peaks including the Matterhorn, Ararat, Kilimanjaro, Fiji, Rainier and the Grand Tetons.
- He followed Marco Polo's route through all of the Middle East, Asia and China.
- He's run a mile in five minutes, broad jumped 15 feet, high jumped five feet and performed 200 sit-ups and 20 pull-ups.
- He was the first person to explore the 4200-mile length of the world's longest river, the Nile. It was the number one goal of his life when he made his original list at 15, and prompted the L.A. Times to name him "The Real Life Indiana Jones" when he achieved it. He has also been down the Amazon, Congo and other major rivers of the world.
- John has been to 122 countries, lived with 260 different tribal groups, and explored the underwater reefs of Florida, the Great Barrier Reef in Australia, the Red Sea, and more.
- He has flown 40 different types of aircraft and still

holds civilian air records; has read the Bible cover to cover and learned to speak French, Spanish and Arabic.

- The last two on his original list included marrying and having children (he has six) and living to see the 21st Century, which he has done in style.

And I'm just getting started. But I think you get the point.

More than just one of the greatest adventurers the world has ever known, Goddard is an incredibly wise person, as this quote of his demonstrates: "If you really know what you want out of life, it's amazing how opportunities will come to enable you to carry them out."

What was John's secret? First, he wrote his dreams down. I'll bet that's something you've heard before. I heard it for twenty years and ignored it too! But the fact is, writing your goals down is powerful, increasing your chances of success by at least 1000% according to Brian Tracy.

John's second secret is that his dreams were BIG. There's no power at all in small dreams. When the dream isn't big enough, it's too easy to give in to the obstacles that appear in our life. It's very difficult to maintain the persistence that all great achievement requires when the dream is small or ordinary.

Achieving big goals requires you to become a bigger person. You must develop new habits, abilities, skills, and attitudes. You must stretch yourself, and in so doing, you will be forever stretched. As legendary coach Lou Holtz said, "if you are bored with life, if you don't get up every morning with a burning desire to do things—you don't have enough goals." Certainly John Goddard has not only chosen plenty of goals to accomplish, he has achieved them, and grown immensely in the process.

Big goal achievers start with lifetime goals. What do you stand for? What would you want people to say about you after you're gone? What sort of legacy do you want to leave behind? What are your values and your moral and ethical beliefs? Let these things push you forward. Let them really shape your life in a positive and powerful way. A definite purpose is the absolute starting point from which to begin. When backed by a burning desire, that purpose takes on a life of its own. Purpose plus desire can be translated into reality. Adopt a definite purpose, and then stand firmly by that purpose, until it easily and naturally becomes an all-consuming obsession!

As Marcus Aurelius said, "only big dreams have the power to move men's souls."

How big is BIG? If it doesn't make you a little nervous — you know that feeling in the pit of your stomach; if it doesn't take your breath away the first time you think about it, it's probably not big enough. Those physical symptoms I just described are the result of a chemical change in your body caused by your thoughts. When your dream is big enough that the thought of it causes your body to undergo physical changes, you're on the right path. You MUST possess a definiteness of purpose in order to win in life. You must know what you want, and you must have a **burning desire** to possess it, for dreams are the seeds of realities.

No more effort is required to dream big, to demand abundance and personal prosperity, than is required to accept poverty and misery. Our only limitations are those we set up in our minds. Strange and imponderable is the power of the human mind! We literally become the result of our own thoughts.

Thoughts of lack and scarcity breed feelings of aggressiveness, selfishness, worry, and jealousy. Its effects are negative. Thoughts of abundance breed feelings of kindness, love, prosperity, and generosity. Its effects are positive. Which thoughts you choose to focus on is entirely up to you.

The brain believes whatever we tell it to believe. What you tell it, it will create. It has no other choice. The brain runs the ship. If you want to make a change, and make it stick, you've got to do it the way the brain works.

Every thought we think, whether conscious or unconscious, is translated by the brain into electrical impulses. These impulses direct our brain's control centers. Thus, every emotion, feeling, action, and moment is directed and controlled by our thoughts.

You can reprogram your brain! You can replace the old negative images and limiting beliefs with positive and productive ones. It's easy! This book will teach you how to do that. Success is never the result of chance, luck, or hard work alone. There are countless numbers of unsuccessful people who work hard. Success is the result of learning definite principles, or "secrets," and applying them consistently in such a way so as to get the result we desire. That's what this book will teach you how to do.

Bringing about change is difficult at first if it's something we haven't done consciously in the past. It takes a great deal of concentration, effort, discipline, and desire. This is why so few people change in great amounts during their lifetime. But perhaps if they knew that there is an infinite amount of power within them, they would be willing, even eager, to change. They merely need to learn how to access this power.

The sun's light, unfocused, is merely warmth; but when those same rays are focused through a magnifying glass, it has the power to burn through paper! This power of focus can also be applied to the imagination. The aimless person's imagination is allowed to wander and provide merely general entertainment. But when this same person's imagination is applied steadfastly with purpose, it can program their self-image, their success mechanism, to achieve whatever that person so chooses.

Success is not limited to those few individuals who have achieved numerous goals and accomplishments, those few who are admired by the world around them. Successful people are those who purposely set bigger goals, goals that stretch them and call for continued growth. A successful person works towards their goals. A successful person enjoys a fulfilled and well-balanced life in the process.

Your potential is unlimited. Your subconscious always says yes to your potential. But it doesn't decide your potential for you. YOU decide! Simply tell your mind what you want and then begin to act on it while keeping your desired result clearly in your mind.

William James was on the right track when he said, "your physical actions are simply the outward manifestation of your inner thoughts. What you see in yourself is what you get out of yourself." What are you choosing to see in yourself? Does it sufficiently represent your utmost potential? Or are you continually selling yourself short?

To change your world, to change your life, you need only

perceive it in a different light. What you "see" in your mind is what you ultimately expect. What you expect is what you ultimately get.

There are no magic powers at work that make some people successful and others failures. "Average" people are average because they think "average" thoughts. "Exceptional" people are exceptional because they think "exceptional" thoughts.

Life gives you whatever you ask for. What are you asking of your life?

NOW IT'S TIME TO TAKE ACTION:

Excercise 1: Set aside time when you can turn outside distractions off and get quiet inside. Use a legal pad (it worked for John Goddard) and review the Dream Triggers on the next page. Meditate a few minutes on each one and write down whatever comes to your mind. Don't worry about whether it's realistic or whether it's a serious dream. You can prioritize your dreams when you're finished.

Dream Starters or Goal Triggers

- ❍ Are you pleased with your physical appearance?
- ❍ When is the last time you exercised? What did you do?
- ❍ What kinds of activities do you enjoy doing with family and friends?
- ❍ How do you spend your solitary time?
- ❍ When is the last time you had a physical?
- ❍ What is the name of the last book you read?
- ❍ How do you spend your Friday nights?
- ❍ What hobbies do you have? When is the last time you participated in any of them?

- ❍ Who are your five closest friends?
- ❍ When is the last time you spent time with them? What did you do?
- ❍ Where do you want to go that you haven't gone?
- ❍ What do you want to see that you haven't seen?
- ❍ What do you want to experience that you haven't experienced?
- ❍ What do you want to do that you haven't done?
- ❍ What do you want to try that you haven't tried?
- ❍ How much time do you spend on/with the people in your organization?
- ❍ Are you more focused on results, people, or productivity?
- ❍ Do you enjoy your job?
- ❍ How well do you manage your time? At work? At home? Socially?
- ❍ Do you regularly take time off?
- ❍ When is the last time you had a vacation? Where did you go?
- ❍ How can you improve your communication skills? (Speaking, writing, and listening)
- ❍ How much time do you spend with your family?
- ❍ Do you really believe quality time is more important than quantity?
- ❍ How can you become more organized?
- ❍ When is the last time you made a new friend?
- ❍ Where did you meet him/her?
- ❍ What is the name of the last new restaurant you ate at?
- ❍ Have you traveled internationally?

○ Where did you honeymoon?

○ If you could have any occupation in the world, what would it be and why?

○ What is the last musical or sporting event you attended?

○ What is the name of the last class you took? When was that?

○ How often have you changed jobs in the last 10 years?

○ How much money do you have in savings/investments?

○ How much do you weigh?

○ What is the last new thing you learned?

○ What is your household net worth?

○ When is the last time you "played?"

○ What trade publications do you subscribe to?

○ What magazines or newspapers do you subscribe to? Do you read them?

○ What organizations or clubs do you belong to? Why did you join?

• • •

Exercise 2: In his book *The Success Principles*, Jack Canfield suggests answering the following questions:

○ Reflect on why you're here.

○ What is your ultimate purpose in life?

○ What do you want to be, do, and have?

○ What do you want to accomplish?

○ What do you want to experience?
○ What possessions do you wish to acquire?
○ What does success look like to you?
○ Make a list of:
○ 30 things you want to do;
○ 30 things you want to have; and
○ 30 things you want to be before you die.

Vague desires and goals produce vague results. Be as clear and detailed as possible. Once you are clear about what you want, keep your mind focused on it. The how will show up.

• • •

Exercise 3: This exercise is in Dr. Daniel Amen's book *Change Your Brain, Change Your Life*. This exercise is called the "One Page Miracle," and will help to guide your thoughts, words, and actions in a positive and goal-oriented way.

Take a sheet of paper and write the following headings:

Relationship
    Spouse
    Children
    Extended Family
    Friends
Work
Money
    Short-Term
    Long-Term

Myself
Body
Mind
Spirit

Next to each subheading, clearly write out what's important to you in that area of your life. Write down what you want. Be positive, and write in the first person. Keep a copy with you so you can work on it over time. Place it where you can see it every day. By looking at it every day, you will consciously focus on what's important to you. You will more easily be able to supervise yourself and match your actions to what you want. Your life will become more conscious, and you will spend more of your time and energy focused on what's important to you.

Secret #2: Understanding the Beginning of All Achievement

In the classic success book, ***Think and Grow Rich***, Napoleon Hill wrote: **"desire is the starting point of all achievement…the first step toward all riches."** And he used these adjectives to describe the kind of desire he found after interviewing 500 of the most successful people of the time: **consuming, obsessive, pulsating and burning**. Can you describe your current desire for your goals with the same words?

Can you remember the feelings you had from the most intense romantic experience of your life? Do you remember how that person was all you thought about, dreamed about and talked about. You couldn't get enough of them. When you weren't in their presence you were on the phone talking to them—sometimes for hours. When you weren't in their presence or talking to them, you were busy planning your next encounter with them. In a word, you were consumed.

Desire is so powerful that people will risk their life, freedom, fortune and everything else in order to satisfy it. Desire can literally be transmuted into gold!

My friend Rene Godefroy left behind the agonizing poverty of Haiti, his native country, to come to the abundance and opportunity of the U.S. It was desire of the strongest kind —*consuming, obsessive, pulsating and burning* – that led him on his journey to freedom by holding on to the underside of a tractor-trailer during a harrowing, five-hour trip that many other immigrants didn't survive.

Chances are you'll never have to risk your life to live your dream, but can you imagine how much more effective you'll be when your desire for your dream is as strong as Rene's was?

Desire says, "I want to," "I can," "I will," "I see opportunity." Between where you are and where you want to be you will find the emotional state of desire. Desire is a positive and magnetic force. Use it to your advantage!

Achievers are people who want to win! They know that only they can make it happen, and are ready and prepared to win, for they know that desire and faith are an indestructible team. These individuals know no such word as impossible. Desire and faith are readily available for anyone and everyone. Their supply is infinite, and they can make anything possible.

"What a different story men would have to tell if only they would adopt a definite purpose, and stand by that purpose until it had time to become an all-consuming obsession!" Hill also noted in ***Think and Grow Rich***.

A burning desire to be someone and to do something is the starting point where dreams take place. Lack of ambition or laziness will not bring birth to your dreams. Mere wishing will not bring riches, either. But once that burning desire is acquired, then planning definite ways to achieve your goals, and being persistent, no matter what might happen will bring you everything that you ask for. So don't give up your desires to anyone. If you had found a buried treasure, you wouldn't readily give it up to whomever were to ask you for it. Don't give up your desires. They are even MORE powerful than gold and money.

Rational thought must be accompanied by deep feeling and desire in order to be effective in changing your beliefs and behaviors. Picture for a moment what you would like to be and have, and assume that such things are possible for you to achieve. Arouse a deep desire for these things. Become enthusiastic about them. Actively engage yourself in these desires! Dwell on them, and keep going over them in your mind. Your desire will begin to activate your subconscious. It will begin to help you carry out the necessary steps to achieve them.

Your present negative beliefs were formed by combining thoughts plus feelings. If you concentrate enough on creating new emotions and feelings, backed by your desires, your new thoughts and ideas will form new pictures, and your previous fears and doubts will be cancelled out. This is the vast importance of desire!

If you are struggling with the area of desire, perhaps you have not yet found the right goal to focus on. One way to tell if you have chosen the right goal is to ask yourself some questions:

Do you regularly and often feel ecstatic about what you are doing?

Do you continually surprise yourself at your improved level of performance?

If your answers to these two questions are no, or you have to really think about it, you more than likely have not yet found your area of excellence. Keep searching until you find something that really sparks your feelings of desire.

If you want to know how to turn your desire into a reality, there are six specific actions to take (these can also be found in *Think and Grow Rich*):

1. Fix in your mind exactly what it is that you want. Be definite and specific.
2. Determine exactly what you intend to give in return for acquiring what you want. (Remember, you can't get something for nothing.)
3. Decide upon a definite date when you intend to achieve what you want, as specified in number one.
4. Create a definite plan for achieving your desire, and begin **IMMEDIATELY**. It doesn't matter if you're ready or not, begin regardless!
5. Write out a clear and concise statement of the goal you intend to achieve. Name the date you will achieve it, what you intend to give in return, and the plan through which you will gain your goal.
6. Read your statement aloud, once upon arising, and once upon retiring at night. As you read, you must **SEE, FEEL**, and **BELIEVE** you are already in possession of that goal. Become so determined to have it that you convince yourself that you WILL have it. Repetition is key!

In his book ***Think Like a Winner***, Dr. Walter Doyle Staples identifies 10 key goal-setting principles:

1. Identify a major goal that is important to you and sufficiently challenging. It should be a goal that can somehow be measured and quantified.
2. Choose an exact date by which you wish to accomplish this goal.
3. Think about and explore various ways you could achieve this goal.
4. Decide upon a detailed action plan to follow. These are

to be actions that will help you acquire necessary knowledge, develop additional skills, and meet people that can assist you in achieving your goal. If you aren't sure of which actions to take, just decide as best as you can.

5. Compile a list of the possible obstacles you will have to overcome in order to reach your chosen goal or destination.

6. List the major benefits you will receive upon reaching this goal.

7. Form a master plan by writing down your answers to the previous six principles.

8. Once in the morning and once at night, read your master plan, out loud, everyday, until you achieve your goal.

9. As you read these statements, see yourself as already achieving your goal. Really be able to believe you've accomplished it. What would it feel like? What would it look like?

10. Whether you're ready or not, begin to implement your plan. If you don't yet feel ready, don't worry, you soon will!

As you perform these tasks, you will be able to recite your goals and action steps upon request. Be able to wake up each day with your goal on the tip of your tongue!

It is the job of your conscious mind to decide what you want, select goals you wish to achieve, and concentrate on what you want. Once you decide what you want, do NOT waste time thinking about what you do NOT want. In other words, don't think about the consequence of failure, which is what you do not want. Just focus on what you want to accomplish, achieve, and receive!

You will begin to receive what you ask for once you become success conscious. It is impossible to achieve what you want while still remaining failure conscious. You must become so consumed with your desire that you are readily able to completely see yourself achieving your goal. You must see yourself already achieving it. How would it feel? Keep this feeling with you at all times. It will help to propel you forward.

NOW IT'S TIME TO TAKE ACTION:

Professional sales people know that they must arouse a prospect's emotion of desire in order to have a chance at closing the sale. Why else do you think it's so important to the salesperson that you take their car for a test drive? They know that the experience can arouse the emotions that create desire. So use the same principle to arouse desire for your dream. Figure out a way to test drive it.

Want a new home? Buy a book or magazine with house designs. Spend the weekends visiting open houses. A friend of mine once built a "to scale" model of the three-story French Provincial he wanted to live in, complete with scaled furnishings. **The more you "stoke" your desire the more it will grow to be *consuming, obsessive, pulsating and burning.***

Secret #3:
What You See is What You Get

WORLD-CLASS ACHIEVERS **have trained themselves to "vision their dream." They see it on the inside long before the world sees it on the outside.** One of my very favorite stories about visioning the dream has to do with Walt Disney's widow. Whenever they were dedicating Epcot a reporter went up to Lillian Disney and said to her that it was a shame that Walt wasn't there to see how everything had turned out. She turned to the reporter without any hesitation and replied, "Oh, he saw it, and long before we ever did." What you see in your mind's eye is what you get, and Walt saw Epcot long before it was built and long before anyone else did.

A key part of visioning your dream is the practice of visualization and there are a number of well-known examples of the power of visualization. None other than golfing legend Jack Nicklaus is said to have always played a course in his mind before actually beginning a game. In his own words: "I never hit a shot, not even in practice, without having a very sharp, in-focus picture of it in my head. First I see the ball where I want it to finish, nice and white and sitting up high on the bright green grass. Then the scene quickly changes, and I see the ball going there; its path, trajectory, and shape, even its behavior on landing. Then there is a sort of fade-out, and the next scene shows me making the kind of swing that will turn the previous images into reality."

One night in 1987, Jim Carrey was a 25-year-old struggling comic when he drove his old Toyota up to Mulholland Drive in the Hollywood Hills. Sitting there overlooking the City of Angels and visioning his future, Carrey wrote himself a check for $10 million. He dated it Thanksgiving 1995 and added the notation, "for acting services rendered."

Carrey stuck the check in his wallet and pulled it out often, especially when things hadn't gone quite like he hoped they would.

This story has become famous, of course, because Carrey's expression of brazen optimism turned out to be conservative. By the time 1995 actually rolled around, his rambunctious goofball roles in "Ace Ventura: Pet Detective," "The Mask" and "Dumb & Dumber" had yielded worldwide grosses of $550 million, and the newly minted superstar's asking price was up to $20 million per picture.

Brian Tracy says that, "All improvement in your life begins with an improvement in your mental pictures. Your mental pictures act as a guidance mechanism that causes you to act in ways that make your mental pictures come true in your life."

The Law of Correspondence says that "As within, so without." It says that your outer world tends to be a reflection of your inner world - like a mirror. What you see in the world around you will be consistent over time with the world inside you. The Law of Concentration says that, "Whatever you dwell upon grows in your reality." Those two laws in combination explain much of success and most of failure.

THE POWER OF VISUALIZATION

Successful people are those who continually think about pictures and images of the person they would like to be and the life they would like to lead. Your subconscious mind is extraordinarily powerful, but it is a servant, not a master. Your subconscious mind coordinates every aspect of your thoughts, feelings, behaviors, words, actions, and emotions to fit a pattern consistent with your dominant mental pictures. It guides you to engage in the behaviors that move you ever closer to achieving the goals you visualize most of the time.

Winners hold onto the image of the person they want to become. Neil Armstrong, the first person in history to ever walk on the surface of the moon, had a vision since he was a child. After his historic voyage to the moon and back, he said, "Ever since I was a little boy, I dreamed that I would do something important in aviation." That vision stuck with him for decades. And it led him to accomplish one of the greatest feats in human history.

The business tycoon Conrad Hilton didn't stumble upon the hotel business haphazardly or by mistake. As a boy, he would play a game where he would imagine he was a hotel operator. When he started in the hotel business, he would buy dilapidated and run down properties, and proceed to restore their unforeseen and hidden beauty. He didn't see their present, unfavorable conditions. He would see the hotel the building would become after its makeover. He would rebuild them as first class properties. By seeing what could be, he turned the dilapidated structure into something valuable to himself, his employees, and his customers.

Make sure you're holding onto an image of yourself that you want, and not one that you don't want. Your behavior and performance are almost always consistent with your self-image. When you constantly and consistently hold the new self-image in your mind, your behaviors and actions will naturally change, helping you create a better you.

In your imagination, you don't ever have to fail! Make winning your habit, simply by simulating winning, in your mind's eye. If you make a mistake, imagine completing the task perfectly. Soon, your subconscious will make your mental practice into a reality. Whatever you imagine in your mind is a preview of what will soon be brought about. You have to provide your subconscious with a new image if you want to bring about change. Otherwise, you will automatically refer back to previous programming, and the goal-achieving process will unnecessarily require more time.

Visualization is the process of forming abstract mental pictures in your mind's eye. You must visualize what you want to happen, the goal you want to reach, and the life you want to be living. Physical sight involves your optic nerve. However, the optic nerve is also directly involved in the visualization process. It's actively participating, just as if you were physically seeing what you're imagining. Your subconscious really DOES think it's happening!

The process of visualization varies from person to person. Some people simply tell themselves, in words, something they want to occur. Not everyone is able to literally see pictures when they visualize. Use the process in a way that works for you.

Simply establish a clearly defined goal, write it down,

and dwell on it, morning and night. Imagine you've already achieved it. Make it as vivid as possible. Add feelings and emotions that you will feel when you accomplish the goal. Your subconscious literally cannot tell the difference between reality and fantasy, truth and a lie. The mind needs specific images. It needs things to direct it. How you direct it is entirely and completely up to you.

When you set a goal, give yourself detailed instructions that specify exactly what you want. Then stand back and get out of the way. Take an active role, but also allow your subconscious to do the work with you. Involve as many senses as you can. Include what you would see, what you would smell, what you would taste, what you would feel, what you would hear, upon performing and accomplishing your goal.

Really live your goals! The more senses you involve, the more your subconscious will work to make your goal happen. Visualization greatly accelerates the achievement of any success. The act of creating vivid and exciting pictures in your mind activates your mind's creativity. You will notice available resources to help you achieve your goals. These are resources you may not have realized had you not been actively visualizing yourself completing your goals. The people and resources needed to achieve your goals will be attracted to you when you regularly visualize!

When you visualize something that you want but don't yet have, a conflict is created between your conscious and subconscious mind. Your subconscious mind actively tries to solve this conflict by helping you to turn your fantasy into reality.

The only limitations are those we set up in our own minds. Our limitations are proportionate to our use or lack of use of our imagination. Many of us haven't used our imagination faculties in years, if not decades. It may have become weak through inaction. However, it can easily be revived.

This faculty doesn't die, it just becomes weakened. Immediately begin to put your imagination to work. Build a plan to transform your desire into reality. Ideas are a critical ingredient of all achievements. Our imaginations specialize in creating ideas to help us achieve whatever it is we wish.

When you see a thing clearly in your mind's eye, your subconscious immediately takes control. It is far more effective at achieving goals than by conscious effort or willpower alone. The exact same hormones and neurotransmitters are used and released when you are visualizing and when you are seeing it in reality.

You don't have to spend a lot of time visualizing. Just 10 to 15 minutes a day is more than enough time to turn your dreams into realities. The prominent speaker Azim Jamal recommends what he calls "the hour of power." He suggests 20 minutes of visualization and meditation, 20 minutes of exercise, and 20 minutes of reading inspirational books. If you spend one hour a day performing the "hour of power," your achievements will skyrocket!

Bruce Jenner, who won the gold medal for the Olympic decathlon, is a prime example of how to use visualization for your success. For two years prior to winning the gold medal, every day he would imagine winning that gold medal he so strongly desired. His brain's connections related to performance and winning were enhanced and made stronger. His body's muscles fired in exactly the same way, every time, whether he was performing mentally or physically. For TWO

YEARS, he imagined winning the gold medal. He ultimately won that gold medal!

Another athlete that used the process of visualization to his advantage is the professional golfer Cory Pavin. He would visualize hitting every golf ball at a specific hole, occurring in a specific tournament. Remember, the more specific, the better! He maintained conscious control over each shot in his mind. He would hit 1000 golf balls every day, in his mind's eye.

He knew that simply physically hitting shot after shot, golf ball after golf ball, day after day, would NOT help him to reach great levels of achievement in the game of golf. Before physically hitting a golf ball, he would visualize EXACTLY where he wanted the golf ball to fall after striking it with his golf club.

A scientific study was done to prove the importance and power of visualization in achieving a task. One group of participants visualized shooting basketballs into a basketball net perfectly. Another group of participants visualized shooting baskets into a net perfectly, and then physically shot basketballs into a basketball net. When the two groups both physically performed shooting basketballs, the group that visualized and then practiced did best.

However, the group that merely visualized shooting perfect baskets performed within 6/10 of one percent of the other group! They merely visualized what they wanted to happen, and performed almost as well as the group that visualized and physically practiced. The statement "practice makes perfect" is NOT true, unless you're visually practicing. Physical practice alone is NOT the best way to achieve your goals!

Before taking any new action, first visualize yourself completing that action perfectly. Your success at the action will skyrocket!

Olympic high diver Greg Louganis reportedly mentally rehearsed each of his dives 40 times immediately prior to the dive!

The well-known and respected preacher Billy Graham didn't begin his career by accident. Before the unknown preacher performed in front of live audiences, he preached sermons to cypress stumps in a Florida swamp, imagining a crowd of avid listeners! Soon, those audiences of stumps were replaced by audiences of millions of people.

Do you think it's a coincidence that these highly successful individuals used visualization on a daily basis? I'll let you answer that question for yourself.

A highly effective exercise involved in the process of visualization is to recall past successes and remember them, in your mind's eye. You merely need an experience where you completed something you wanted to complete and felt satisfaction and reward.

If you can remember these feelings from the past, they will be reactivated in the present, the here and now. Because self-confidence is built on memories of past successes, recalling these experiences will help you to feel self-confident towards achieving new goals. Apply these same feelings to what you're achieving NOW. Your subconscious will believe that you're achieving these things now, just as it completed tasks in the past. The more an image is activated or replayed, the more powerful it becomes.

Sometimes we set a goal, even if we don't yet know how to achieve that goal. Trust that your subconscious will help you come up with a solution to your problem or task at hand. It is likely to give you solutions at the most unlikely times and places, such as the shower or while sleeping.

You MUST take ACTIVE and conscious control when solutions are presented to you. These solutions, created by your subconscious, are immediately placed in your short-term memory. The average time that a thought remains in the short-term memory is 37 SECONDS! After that, it ceases firing. Once it's gone, it's gone. Have you ever had it happen where you thought, "Oh, this idea is so good, there's no way that I will forget it!" You fail to TAKE ACTION on the thought, and next thing you know, you forget the idea. It's gone and you can't get it back, no matter how hard you try!

Fortunately, you CAN take control and place the idea, or thought, into long-term memory. There are three ways to do this:

1. Repetition: Repeating the idea you want to remember creates more thought connections and increases the level of importance your brain places on that idea. Repetition is the key to real learning according to Jack Canfield, the co-author of the Chicken Soup for the Soul series.

2. Association: Connect that idea with something else in your brain. That way, both will be stored in your brain.

3. Trauma: A traumatic or VERY important experience is automatically placed into your long-term memory. For example, most everyone remembers where they were on 9/11 when terrorists attacked the U.S.

Or, you can do the simplest action of all: WRITE THE IDEA DOWN! Or you can say the idea into an audio recorder and save it for future use. If you do these simple steps, you will never regret letting a good idea escape you. You are taking control of your thoughts, and thus taking control of your actions and ultimately your life!

THE IMPORTANCE OF SELF-TALK

Another important key to setting and accomplishing goals is the practice of positive self-talk. What you continually feed your subconscious will ultimately be what you acquire. If you feed your subconscious with negative images and words, you will obtain those very things you say you do not want.

Luckily, this process can easily be used to your benefit. If you feed your subconscious with positive images and words, those fantasy images soon will become reality! All you have to do is erase and replace! Your own programmed self-talk lies at the very root of your success, or of your failure for that matter.

Positive thinking helps to create a new reality. This new reality will be more consistent with positive behavior and higher levels of performance. The well-known author and speaker Zig Ziglar exemplifies this fact through his statement, "change your thoughts and you change your world."

In order to motivate someone to do something, you must influence their emotions. Someone will not outwardly do something they will not even do internally. Our emotions are our main motivators. Before the new action can take place, we must change and redirect our emotions regarding that action. This is true whether in regards to someone else or yourself.

Instead of looking outward for someone or something to motivate us, how much easier it would be for us to turn inward and use ourselves for our own motivation! If we learn the right words to use when talking to ourselves, we can easily learn to give ourselves the necessary motivation, any time we need it, in order to accomplish our goals. Our best resource is right here within us!

Anything you say out loud or silently to yourself, or to someone else about yourself, is part of your self-talk. What you actively say out loud or silently **automatically**, and with no required effort on your part, sends images to your subconscious mind. Saying "I am tired" or "I hate my job" cannot possibly make you feel better! However, there is a more effective way to talk to yourself, a way that will improve your life for the better.

Positive self-talk is a way to override our past negative programming by replacing it with different, more positive directions. It is a way to take active control of our lives, rather than passively letting life happen to us. Self-talk gives our subconscious mind specific directions and tells it what to work on.

You must actively control the language that you use towards yourself and towards others. Winners rarely berate themselves or put themselves down. Winners use positive self-talk and feedback everyday. They know that by doing so, they will be that much closer to achieving their goals.

As long as you continually complain about your circumstances and life situation, your mind will continue to focus on those things. By continually focusing on the things you don't want, those same thoughts are firing, and you're sending out the same thought vibrations to the Universe. You will continue to attract those same things into your life.

To change this self-defeating cycle, you must focus instead on thinking about, writing about, and talking about the life you want to create for yourself. You must flood your consciousness with the life you want to be living. 80% of lottery winners become bankrupt within five years because they never developed a millionaire mindset. They ultimately ended up at their old comfort zone.

In *What to Say When You Talk to Yourself*, Shad Helmstetter identifies four levels of self-talk.

The first level of self-talk is the level of negative acceptance. This is self-talk by which you say something negative about yourself and accept it.

An example of negative acceptance is the statement, "I can't." Negative acceptance statements are full of doubts, fears, and worries. We can say them out loud, silently, to ourselves, or to another person. How we say it doesn't matter. Even if someone else says them to us, our subconscious still hears them. It makes no difference how seemingly harmless the statements may be. They are the supporting backbone of everything that prevents us from living the life we want to live. These statements keep us stuck where we are, right in our comfort zone. Level one self-talk represents our misgivings, and even our deepest and darkest fears.

The following are examples of NEGATIVE self-talk. More than likely, you've said these following statements before:

I can't remember names.

I'm not creative.

I know it's not going to work, so I'm not going to even bother trying!

Things never work out right for me.

Things never go my way.

The list is endless. You probably thought of some more examples while reading just these five statements.

Did you know that the average person, by the time they're 18, has heard the statement "No, you can't," 160,000 times? How many times do you think they've heard, "Yes, you can?" A mere 10,000 times!!! Do you think this has an impact on your brain, on your subconscious, and your beliefs? You bet it ABSOLUTELY does!

Imagine sitting at your computer's keyboard and typing these sorts of negative commands into your computer. Imagine that you have complete control over your computer, and it does whatever you tell it to do. Pretty soon, it would shut down and you would be unable to get it to do anything productive.

Unfortunately, this is precisely what happens when we say negative statements to ourselves. It's no wonder things don't go the way we want them to! You can't possibly be successful if you program your brain with negative images and statements. It would be like telling a dog to sit and expecting him to lie down. He'll only do what you tell him to do.

Complaining is a common type of level 1 self-talk. It is absolutely amazing the number of people that will complain endlessly about things which they can do nothing about! You have no more control over the weather than you do of a company's present stock price. Complaining about anything outside of your control is senseless and has a DIRECT effect on how we function that day, both physically and mentally.

Level 2 self-talk is the level of recognition and of the need to change. "I need to" and "I should" are statements found in this level of self-talk. Unfortunately, these statements actually work against us! Why? Because the subconscious recognizes that there is a problem to be solved, but it creates no solution at this level. When you are saying, "I need to lose weight," you're REALLY saying, "I need to lose weight…because I'm unhealthy and unattractive!" The sentence you begin at this level is ALWAYS completed by a level 1 statement whether you are conscious of it or not.

Instead of giving birth to dreams, goals, and feelings of accomplishment, level 2 self-talk creates guilt, disappointment, and acknowledgement of our self-created inadequacies.

Level 3 self-talk is the first level of self-talk that begins to work FOR you instead of against you. In this level, you not only recognize a need to change, you decide to do something about it. You state the decision in the present tense, as though the change has already taken place. "I never watch 5 hours of television a day" and "I never let my home get disorganized and messy" are examples of level 3 self-talk statements. In this level, you are automatically telling your subconscious that you want to make a positive change in your life.

You are telling your subconscious to get moving towards a more positive life direction. You are placing the "cannot's" behind you and instead are stating them in a more positive way. Your subconscious begins to work FOR you when you begin to tell it to do so! It will begin to go to work, carrying out its new directions and orders. Just simply learn to tell it in the right way.

Level 4 self-talk is the level of the better you. This level of self-talk is the most effective self-talk we can ever use. This level is used the least, and needed the most. At this level, you are painting a completed new picture of yourself, the way you really want to be, handing it over to your subconscious. You're saying to your subconscious, "This is the me that I want to be! Forget the old programming I was giving to you. This is your new program. Now, let's get to work!"

At level 4, you deal with problems and opportunities in an effective and productive way. Past problems are turned around, and you begin creating new daily successes. You replace "I cannot" with "Yes I can!" Level 4 self-talk is the type of self-talk that encourages, excites, and pushes us forward, towards our goals and dreams. Every negative self-talk statement has a positive, effective self-talk statement.

Now that you are aware of the four different levels, immediately stop using levels 1 and 2, and begin using levels 3 and 4. Turn your level 1 self-talk into more effective level 4 self-talk.

Listen to what you say when you talk, whether to yourself or to others. Is your self-talk predominantly positive or negative? If you have never tried this before, it's a very revealing exercise. You may be surprised at what you hear yourself saying. Once you know what you've been saying, you're more able to change it for the better, in a way that will HELP you rather than harm you.

The majority of people never decide to take control of their thinking. They simply let their thoughts drift, with no particular focus or intent. Their thoughts are echoes of their past programming, beliefs, and perceptions. Their lives reflect this carelessness. Henry Ford knew this fact, for he said, "thinking is the hardest work there is, which is the probable reason why so few [people] engage in it."

Start to practice thinking. Observe your thinking. Begin to be aware of what you're thinking about. Become an expert on knowing how you tend to think. Become an observer of your own thinking patterns. What are you telling your mind? We have in our lives EXACTLY what we have been telling our brain that we want. It's vitally important that you guide your brain's thinking. Change your thinking for the better!

Listen to what you're saying to yourself. If it's working against you, turn it around. Start using self-talk that works FOR you! If you are used to level 1 and 2 self-talk, it may be uncomfortable and challenging when you begin using more effective self-talk. This is normal. If you don't have anything to replace the negative statements with, your mind will return to the negative statements by default. Therefore, practice positive self-talk everyday, and soon it will be second nature!

Instead of creating a negative image, you can create a positive image any time you choose. Simply begin with your self-talk. When you rid yourself of your level 1 self-talk statements, you will have rid yourself of your greatest enemy.

Take control of your thoughts! It will literally change your life. Control your thoughts, and you will control your behavior. You don't have to waste time changing old thoughts. Just start thinking new ones! Repeat positive thoughts again and again. Be repetitive. Your thoughts go down the pathway of least resistance. The more times you think a certain thought, the easier it becomes to think that thought again. So make sure you're repeatedly thinking positive thoughts, thoughts that will help you to achieve your goals. Even if you don't believe the thoughts now, keep repeating them. You soon WILL believe them!

Your thoughts are real things! They form connections in your brain. These connections are not set in stone. You can change them! Connections begin to atrophy within a few days after they have not been used. If you have been thinking thoughts of failure, simply stop thinking them, and in time those connections will lose their power. The connections will lose their strength, become more rigid, and will be less likely to be thought again. Start thinking new, positive thoughts, and they will gain strength over the negative thoughts.

An easy way to gain the most benefit from thinking in a new and positive way is to think these thoughts in a different way each time. For example, instead of always repeating, "I like myself today and everyday," you could vary it to also say, "Everyday I like myself," "I take pride in myself," "I like being me," etc. Also vary the inflection of the statements. Sometimes you can emphasize the first word, sometimes the last word, and so on. This step may seem extremely simple, but sometimes the simplest things are the most effective.

Fire these thoughts with emotion! Really start to put energy and enthusiasm into them! Thoughts that are fired the most, with emotion, are relied upon the most in future events and circumstances. These thoughts will be used the most when making decisions, solving problems, and deciding what actions to take. You want to make sure you are relying upon thoughts that will HELP you along your path of achievement.

Also begin to listen to the self-talk of those around you. Listen to what they say about themselves, others, and the situations they are faced with. Actively seeing how other peoples' negative self-talk affects them and those around them is a very effective and easy way to see how self-talk really DOES control and affect our lives. Look for signs of who is in control of that person's life. Who or what is controlling them? Is it their spouse? Is it their self-image? You can't control what someone else says, but you CAN see how it affects them, whether for better or worse.

YOU HAVE THE CHOICE to view any situation any way you want. It is perfectly okay to be dissatisfied with any area in your life. However, endlessly complaining about the situation you are unhappy about will NOT improve the situation!

If you find yourself falling into this trap of complaining, simply step aside. Monitor your self-talk. Think of more positive and constructive ways to improve what you are saying to yourself and to others. This book will give you some exercises that you can actively use to begin to improve your self-talk and ultimately your life.

James Allen said it well when he stated, "you are today where your thoughts have brought you. You will be tomorrow where your thoughts take you." Where are *your* thoughts taking *you*?

EXAMPLES OF POSITIVE SELF-TALK

- Today and every day, I have a positive mental attitude.
- Today and every day, I believe in myself. I believe I am capable of great things!
- Today I accept full responsibility for my actions and for my life's circumstances. They are a direct result of my past and current thinking.

- Today and every day, I manage my time effectively. I use every minute to its fullest advantage.
- Today and everyday, I value my physical, mental, and spiritual health. I always take good care of myself.
- Today and everyday, I am a highly creative being. I recognize all of life's amazing possibilities.
- I always accomplish tasks fully and with excellence.
- Everyday and in every way, I am getting better and better.
- I like keeping myself fit and looking good.
- I have more energy and stamina than ever before.
- I always do what is best for myself and for my future.
- I am able to reach any goal which I set for myself.
- I enjoy exercising regularly.
- People enjoy being around me. I have self-confidence and self-respect.
- I always choose positive thoughts and statements.
- I commit only to those responsibilities which I know I can fulfill.
- I approve of who I am.
- I am positive, confident, and radiate good things.
- I smile a lot. I am happy on the inside and on the outside.
- I am organized and in control of my life.
- I control my goals and the achievement of my goals.
- Large sums of money come to me quickly and easily.
- I have more money than I need to do everything I wish to do.
- Money comes to me in many unforeseen ways.

- I am making positive choices about what to do with my money and my time.
- Everyday, my income increases whether I am working, playing, or sleeping.
- All of my investments are profitable.
- I can do anything I believe I can do, and I believe I can do anything!

Remember, you can place ANY idea into your subconscious through repetition. Involve your senses and emotions, and the affirmation will be even that much stronger.

ALWAYS state positive self-talk in the present tense. Our subconscious takes every picture as real. When you say, "Don't spill the milk," the subconscious only sees you spilling the milk! Always state positive self-talk as though it has already happened, as though it has already taken place and has been accomplished. Your subconscious can only relate to the present state. Doing this simple step sends a very strong message to your subconscious. You are sending it a completed picture of the accomplished task.

You are presenting your brain's control center with the command that says, "This is what I want you to create for me. This is how I want to be." The more specific and complete the picture, the more specific the directions you are giving to your subconscious mind. When you repeatedly see yourself achieving a goal in your mind's eye, you will consciously begin to believe that you can really achieve it!

A pessimist says, "I'll believe it when I see it."

An optimist says, "I'll see it when I believe it."

That's pretty powerful stuff!

An optimist isn't someone that always thinks positively.

That's physiologically impossible! Rather, an optimist is someone who knows how to interrupt, intercept, and stop negative thoughts before they can be completed. They turn negative thoughts into positive thoughts. You don't have to change HOW you think, simply change WHAT you think.

You can choose to practice positive self-talk silently or out loud. Keep in mind, practicing it out loud may feel and sound silly, but it is FAR more effective and works much more quickly if it is done OUT LOUD! When you talk out loud, more of your senses are involved. More of you becomes involved, and more of you goes to work on improving yourself. You are forcing yourself to put your thoughts into words. You are able to better clarify your thinking and become more specific. Thoughts aren't as readily able to simply drift into your mind. You're taking active control over your thinking when you talk out loud.

Adding emotion while talking to yourself out loud will dramatically strengthen the power of the resulting thoughts. The thoughts will be longer lasting and more easily recalled in the future. When created with strong emotion, the thoughts have more difficulty atrophying. You're more likely to use them again in future circumstances when you need them most.

A GREAT and EXTREMELY powerful exercise is to practice your positive self-talk statements in front of a mirror. Repeat the statements 4 times, each time with more enthusiasm and belief. Even if the belief is forced and false, your subconscious won't know the difference!!! Repeat the statement 4 times in a row, 3-4 times a day, in front of different mirrors preferably, and you will be AMAZED at the results.

Another exercise is to say positive statements to yourself while you're in the shower. We tend to be relaxed while taking a bath or shower, and so it is the perfect environment to practice positive self-talk. When you step into the shower, say out loud, "Good morning!" Really say it with a smile. Tell yourself just how great the day is going to be. Say positive statements, such as, "I am having a GREAT day today! Everything is going my way today! I feel great, I look great, and the world is treating me great! I like myself, and everyone naturally likes me!"

This kind of self-talk will immediately begin to turn your day from an average day into a powerful and productive day. It really works! If you're skeptical, ask yourself if your other habits are working for you or against you. How many positive habits do you really have? If you need some more positive ones, these positive self-talk exercises REALLY DO WORK. Don't take my word for it, try it yourself!

Just the simple act of telling yourself you're going to have a good day, for example, will convince you mentally that you WILL have a good day. Not only that, but also telling yourself this positive statement automatically and unconsciously begins to set off chemical reactions in your brain. These triggers affect your mental state, which affects how you feel, and ultimately how you think for the rest of the day.

One negative event, especially when it's first thing in the morning, can cause an automatic chain reaction that affects the rest of the day, sometimes without even our knowledge. This negative chain of events isn't caused by the problem itself. The problem began with how you responded to the problem. The thought of the circumstance brought an emotional response, which brought a physiological response, then another thought, then another emotional response, and so on. The cycle goes on and on, until you ACTIVELY choose to interrupt it.

Self-write is another effective form of positive self-talk. In self-write, you write down the specific statements and instructions that you want to send to your subconscious mind. By writing your self-talk down, you are actively increasing your awareness of what you want. You become more interested, which naturally creates more energy. It naturally follows that the more energy you put into something, the better the chances of it working for you.

If you want to improve your life—lose weight, earn more money, whatever the goal may be—you MUST first see yourself as worthy and capable of accomplishing your goals. If you don't yet feel worthy or capable, begin right here by changing your self-talk. If you try to accomplish your goal before you even believe you can do it, you will have a very difficult time achieving your goal. If you first begin to change the picture of yourself from a negative picture to a positive picture, your subconscious will actually go to work and HELP you achieve what you are aiming to achieve! It's a pretty miraculous process. Start with your programming, and the rest will follow naturally.

The mind that has gotten rid of the negative talk, and now abounds in positive statements and images, is the most fertile ground one can ever find for growth and achievement. The more positive energy and effort you put forth into an endeavor, the better the chances that the effort will work for you. Anyone can use self-talk and benefit from its results. Decide to benefit from positive self-talk!

The human brain will do anything that you tell it to do, if you tell it often enough and strongly enough! The subconscious sees no difference between the statement that you are clumsy and the statement that you are graceful. It doesn't know the difference between being poor and wealthy. It accepts whatever images and programs you give to it.

One phrase of self-talk can have a positive effect on your behavior and ultimately on your life. But when you paint a new picture of yourself, of the life you want to create, plus positive statements, you will REALLY begin to obtain the benefits of positive self-talk. So make sure you practice positive self-talk while creating a new improved visual image in your mind of the life you want to create. These two are powerful practices that go hand in hand with achievement and success!

Your subconscious works tirelessly and effortlessly to create the life that you imagine. It creates the person that you have described yourself to be. It creates the life that you have imagined yourself to be living. It can ONLY do what you TELL it to do!

Your nervous system literally cannot tell the difference between a real and an imagined experience. It reacts appropriately and effortlessly to whatever you believe to be true. The terms thought, believed, and imagined are synonymous. They are all the same to your nervous system. You can use this fact to your advantage by changing your thoughts and projected images!

When you begin to turn your negative statements to positive statements, your old conditioning and programming will try to stop you.

When you first start the process, make the decision to keep going, no matter what your mind might say! If you know what to expect, you'll be that much more likely to persist. You can even make a statement such as, "I am doing what is best for me. I am confidently and effectively reprogramming my mind." You may feel foolish in the beginning, but the benefits of practicing positive self-talk will quickly outweigh the embarrassment and foolishness you may have felt initially.

In ***What to Say When you Talk to Yourself***, there is a checklist that you can use to determine whether or not your self-talk is going to work for you or against you:

1. Make sure your self-talk is stated in the present tense. You want the picture you are creating in your mind to be a complete picture of you already having accomplished what you are setting out to accomplish. Doing this simple step will help you to get to where you want to be.

2. Make your statements specific. Be as detailed as possible. Vague statements and pictures lead to vague results. You'll be less likely to receive exactly what you want. The more specific you are about your goals, the more specific the directions you will be giving to your subconscious.

3. Make sure your self-talk and images direct you to achieve what you want in a positive and healthy way. Otherwise, your subconscious could use unhealthy or dangerous means to help you get what you want. It doesn't know the difference between right and wrong. For example, if you want to lose 20 pounds, your subconscious could help you lose the weight by giving you

the flu. You would lose the weight, but you would be miserable in the meantime! Make sure your statements and pictures emphasize the importance of your physical and mental health. See yourself happily achieving your goal.

4. Simple self-talk is the best kind of self-talk. You don't want your self-talk to be complicated or complex. You want your self-talk to be easy to remember and recall. You're less likely to use it if it's not easy to remember when you need it.

5. The images you create should be practical and possible for you to achieve. Don't immediately begin expecting and demanding miracles of yourself. If you're earning $25,000, it may be impractical for you to earn $1,000,000 extra in a month's time. It can be done, but you more than likely won't REALLY believe you can achieve it. If you program yourself to achieve the impossible, you will only create frustration and failure. Once you begin achieving attainable goals, you will gain confidence and energy.

6. Be honest with yourself. Acknowledge and recognize previous things that stood in your way of achieving what you wanted to accomplish. Accept where you are now, and decide where you want to go from there.

7. Make sure your self-talk asks the best of you. Don't sell yourself short. Your self-talk should stretch you and help you to grow in a positive manner. Allow your self-talk to pull the best out of you. Allow it to motivate you and help you emerge a winner.

Most motivation simply doesn't stay with you. As soon as you finish with the external motivation, you go back to your old ways. It just doesn't last. This is because the only TRUE motivation is INTERNAL motivation. You can be your own motivator and bring control to your life by activating your own internal coach. Your internal coach is your strongest cheerleader and your best supporter. It will give you direction, bring you newfound purpose, and strengthen your belief. It can never fail you, because it's a part of you!

Your self-talk is the determining factor in whether you're a winner or a loser in life. Your own self-talk is your best form of inner strength and determination. Begin to call your inner resources to action! Put them to work FOR you, rather than against you. You can do it!

Speak to yourself as though you are the single most important person in the whole Universe. You are!

In time, positive self-talk will become as natural and effortless as walking, eating, and sleeping, IF you are consistent and practice it every day. When positive self-talk becomes a habit, successes naturally occur. Once positive self-talk is mastered, you will have given yourself one of the greatest gifts imaginable.

When we improve ourselves internally, our lives improve naturally and automatically. The things you wish to acquire are gained much more easily and readily. Improve yourself, and you will improve your life. You must become successful on the inside if you ever want to become successful on the outside.

NOW IT'S TIME TO TAKE ACTION:

Exercise 1: Begin to make a list of your past and present self-talk. You can spend as little or as much time on this exercise as you choose. Even just 20 to 30 minutes of examining your self-talk will be very revealing to you. What are the ten most significant and frequent self-talk statements you say to yourself, whether silently or out loud? Keep working on this until you have ten statements. Most of us have literally dozens of negative statements we say to ourselves frequently.

If you are not used to monitoring your thoughts and writing things down, just becoming conscious of your thoughts and your self-talk will help you to achieve positive and desirable results. However, choosing positive replacements for your negative self-talk will be easier if you write them out.

The more aware you are of what you say to yourself, the easier it will be for you to replace these statements with more effective and goal-oriented statements. Once you're aware of where your positive and negative programming comes from, it will be much easier for you to change your programming to your advantage. You will be able to take full responsibility and thus gain better control over your life.

• • •

Exercise 2: This exercise is presented by Jack Canfield in his book *The Success Principles*. Use these nine guidelines to help you create effective affirmations:

1. Start your affirmation with the words **"I am."** These

two words are the most powerful words in the English language. The word OM, said to be the first uttered word in the Universe's existence, translates into these two words. The subconscious takes any sentence that starts with "I am" and interprets it as a command, as something it needs to make happen.

2. Use the present tense. Describe what you want as though you already have it. Phrase it in a way that makes it sound as though it's already been accomplished.

3. State the affirmation in the positive. You must affirm what you want and NOT what you don't want.

4. Keep the statement brief. You want the statement to be memorable.

5. Make it specific. Vague affirmations tend to produce vague results.

6. Include an action word ending in "-ing," such as "seeing" versus "see." The active verb adds power by seeming as though the action is being taken right now, in the present.

7. Include at least one dynamic emotion or feeling word. What is the emotional state you will be feeling upon achieving your goal? Some possible words are enjoying, happily, celebrating, etc.

8. Make affirmations for yourself, not for others. They should describe your own behavior, and not others' behaviors. You can only control your own actions. Don't waste time trying to change or control the behaviors of other people.

9. Add "or something better." Sometimes we limit

ourselves, and don't see something better available to us. Let your affirmations include this phrase.

Visualize what you want to create, place yourself inside the picture, and see things through your eyes. Hear the sounds you will hear upon accomplishing this goal. Feel the feeling you will feel. Describe what you're experiencing.

• • •

Exercise 3: This exercise can be found in ***The New Psycho-Cybernetics***. It will help you to create a new self-image based on goals you wish to achieve.

Your present self-image was built out of pictures that you programmed into your subconscious. These pictures emerged as a result of how you interpreted and evaluated past experiences.

Now you will use the same method to create a new and more adequate self-image to take the place of your current inadequate one. Pick a goal you wish to achieve, whether in the near future, or the long-term.

Set aside a period of time each day (preferably the same time each day), where you can be alone and undisturbed. Relax and make yourself as comfortable as possible. Close your eyes, and begin to exercise your imagination. Make these pictures as vivid and detailed as possible. Pay attention to small details, sights, sounds, and objects in your imagined environment. You are creating a practice experience, and details are vitally important. Your nervous system will see this created image as just as real as an actual experience when you make this created image as detailed as possible. The more detailed, the better!

See yourself acting and reacting appropriately, successfully, the way you would want to actually act when you achieve this goal. It doesn't matter how you have acted or reacted in the past. You don't need to try to have faith that you will act appropriately in the future. Your nervous system will take care of that—if you continue to practice.

See yourself acting and performing as you want to be. Imagine how you would feel if you were achieving what you want to achieve, if you had the personality you need in order to achieve this event you're imagining. If you're shy and timid, see yourself as acting confident, poised, elegant, and attractive. See yourself behaving courageously.

This exercise builds new memories and brain connections into your central nervous system. After practicing it everyday, consistently, you will begin to find yourself acting differently, in accordance with your image, as though it's automatic and spontaneous. Your central nervous system will begin to act in accordance with your new self-image. Soon, your old self-image will be a thing of the past. It will be replaced with your new self-image, without you forcing it to.

You can also write out this picture, this goal that you wish to create in the future. Make it as detailed as possible. Writing it out will help you to maintain your focus on the task at hand. While effective, visualization can be difficult to maintain. Our mind wanders readily and quickly when we drop focus for a split second. As you write out your picture, you are forming it in your mind simultaneously.

Play and enjoy this mental scene everyday for as long as you wish, until you achieve it! Along the way, you may even create a bigger goal and a bigger vision. You may find that you sold yourself far too short!

This process is about creating a positive self-image and using your inner resources to help you achieve that self-image. The statements you've repeatedly said to yourself are not set in stone. You DON'T have to keep repeating them! Feelings of inferiority or inadequacy or inability originate from conclusions we ourselves have drawn from our past experiences.

Your objective is to replace these negative and ineffective feelings and images with more positive and effective feelings and images. You want to help to develop yourself in a unique and beneficial way, for the benefit of yourself and others.

You can literally lie your way to higher success and achievement levels! Act your way to higher success and achievement. If you want to be less shy, you can act less shy! If you keep acting confident for a minimum of 21 days, you'll form enough new thought connections that your acting confident soon becomes real! You'll be the confident person you always wished you could be.

Act like a motivated and successful person would act. Act as if you are already where you want to be. Think like, talk like, dress like, act like, and feel like the person who has achieved what you want to achieve. This acting "as if" sends powerful messages to your subconscious mind. It will help to create ways to help you achieve your goals. The Universe will see that this goal is something that you REALLY want. You will draw to yourself the necessary resources.

You'll soon turn into a motivated and successful person,

someone that others look to and admire! Stimulating your brain in this way forms new connections, and when repeated enough, the new images become placed on your brain's "important list." This list directly influences your feelings and actions. "Fake it 'til you make it" takes on new meaning. Fake your way to the top, and soon you will BE at the top! Harness the power of visualization.

• • •

Exercise 4: Use a dream board. It's one of the best ways to begin to vision your future. You can put any picture you want on your board. It could be a picture of a beluga whale encounter at SeaWorld. It could be pictures of famous athletes with your head attached to their body. It could be dates for a trip to Panama. Use whatever it takes to help you see what you want to achieve.

Your dream board doesn't have to be anything fancy. It could be as simple as pictures placed on your computer credenza. You can allow these pictures to be in your peripheral vision when you're at your desk.

Put pictures of what you want all throughout your house, your workplace, even your car! One personal development speaker placed on his car's dashboard a picture of the woman he wanted to marry. Months later, he was in fact married to that woman! When you place pictures of what you want in places where you will definitely see them, more brain connections and brain cells will be created related to those things.

Your subconscious will help you to notice ways and methods to help you get what you want.

You can also create a "dream book." Buy a 3 ring binder, a scrapbook, or a journal. Use a separate page for each of your goals. Write the goal at the top of the page. Illustrate and describe the goal with pictures, words, phrases, anything that will help you to imagine it. As new goals and desires emerge, create a new page and add them to your dream book. Review the pages everyday, preferably at least 2-3 times a day.

• • •

Exercise 5: This next exercise can also be found in ***The New Psycho-Cybernetics***. It is a five step process that will help you learn how to use your subconscious to your best advantage.

1. AIM: Your subconscious must have a goal or target. The goal you choose must be seen as already achieved or in existence. If you see it as not yet achieved, it will take you and your subconscious that much longer to achieve it.

2. TRUST: The subconscious, or automatic mechanism, works best when given specific goals or results to work towards. If the means to achieve the goal isn't yet apparent, do not be discouraged. The means will most often appear when you simply trust and think in terms of the end result that you want to achieve.

3. RELAX: If you make a mistake or fail temporarily, do not be discouraged! Your subconscious achieves a goal by receiving negative feedback, or by going forward, making mistakes, and immediately correcting its course. It learns from failure! Welcome failure. It doesn't mean YOU'RE a failure unless you quit. If you quit, you surely will never achieve what you want!

4. LEARN: Trial and error is essential when learning any new skill or endeavor. You must mentally correct your aim after an error in your mind's eye. Imagine yourself achieving what you are setting out to accomplish. Forget the past effort and move on. Your subconscious will work to imitate the successful performance you imagined in your mind's eye. As the target gets clearer, the subconscious works more efficiently and effectively.

5. DO: You MUST learn to trust your subconscious to do its work. Don't become too concerned or anxious as to whether or not it will work. Don't attempt to control it with too much conscious effort. It works best when you let it work, rather than making it work.

Your subconscious operates below the level of consciousness; therefore, you can never really know how it operates. By its very nature, it operates spontaneously, accepting the feedback and information that is constantly being presented to it. Therefore, you have no advance guarantee. It operates as you act and place a demand on it.

Act as if the proof of your success is already there. Don't wait to act until you have proof; act, and then you will receive the proof! As Emerson said, "Do the thing, and then you will have the power." You will gain energy and focus as you take action; it's simultaneous!

Repeat your goals 2 to 3 times a day. Really take time to

read your goals. Use passion and enthusiasm, while reading your goals out loud. Engage all of your senses. Take a few seconds to imagine how it will feel when you accomplish those goals. See them as already achieved.

Secret #4:
Learning to Believe

SECRET #4 IS, NO DOUBT, the number one secret of World-Class Achievers. When all other things are equal, it's the reason why one person makes millions and the other one can barely make a living. It's the power of belief. The Russian novelist Anton Chekhov stated, "Man is what he believes." It is through your beliefs that you inevitably create the world you live in.

It was a change in my beliefs that turned my life around. In 1997, after we'd been evicted from our home and lost our last automobile, I was at a seminar when I heard 13 magic words: "the size of your success is determined by the size of your belief." I instantly knew that belief was the last piece of the puzzle and I created a plan and began a program to change my beliefs (I later put those exercises into a program called *Can You Believe It?* that has helped thousands around the world harness the power of belief).

Within 90 days changes began occurring in my life. Within six months I achieved national recognition from the sales company I was with at the time. And within one year I was earning a six-figure income. Years later I regularly have days where I earn more income than I earned in all of 1997 put together. All of it was as a result of changing my beliefs.

Napoleon Hill said that faith was the most powerful force on earth (faith is belief without proof). Christians know that the power of faith has been described as being so powerful that a tiny amount (the size of a mustard seed) could move mountains.

Belief is nothing more than what we accept as true or real. Now here's something important to understand: what we accept as true may not be true and it may not be real. But if we accept it as true or real it influences our decisions just as if it were. Life is of our own imagination. It can be a living miracle, or a living nightmare.

From the days of the Greeks and the very first Olympics, it was debated whether a human being could run a sub-four minute mile. The medical and scientific community said that it was not possible. They said if a person ran a mile that fast, their heart would explode. So if you are an athlete out there in training and the medical community says if you break that barrier, your heart is going to explode, do you think that belief might affect your training?

For thousands of years it was a widely held belief that a sub-four minute mile was not only impossible, it was dangerous. Then a medical student named Roger Bannister came along in the 1950's. In England he was studying anatomy and physiology as part of his medical studies and in the process looked at the medical evidence against a sub-four minute mile.

Roger Bannister looked at the evidence and the evidence told him that not only would the heart not explode, but the body of a human being was more than capable of achieving that mark. He convinced himself from the evidence. He changed his belief from that of the held belief and then he actually went out and boldly told the world, "I am going to break the four minute barrier."

Most everyone knows that in 1956, he went out and ran a mile in three minutes and 59.4 seconds and broke the record. Now here's what a lot of people do not know. Within two weeks, another person broke the sub-four minute barrier. In the same year that he did, nine other people ran a mile under four minutes. In thousands of years of recorded history, no one had been able to run a four-minute mile, and in one year, nine people did. What changed? The human body or the human belief?

Evidence is so important when you're trying to change your beliefs. If you took all of your limiting beliefs and searched for the evidence to support them, you wouldn't find any. For instance, take the limiting belief that "it takes money to make money." If you studied the evidence you'd find that belief is false. There are simply too many examples of people who had little or no money who created a fortune (I'm one of them—so I know there's no evidence for that).

One of my limiting beliefs for many years was that my financial success was limited because I had dropped out of college before getting a degree. So let's study the evidence of whether a college degree is required for financial success. You wouldn't have to look too far to find the evidence. One of the richest people in the world, Bill Gates, dropped out of college without a degree. So that belief is obviously false.

Your beliefs create your self-image. Your self-image literally controls what you believe you can or cannot accomplish. It controls what you think is difficult or easy. Your beliefs are just like the thermostat in your home. If you set the thermostat to 72 degrees and turn your air conditioner on, the thermostat will make sure that the temperature in your home never goes over 72 before it directs the air conditioner to begin working.

If you've been struggling with trying to increase your income but you just can't seem to increase it by a significant amount, it's probably because of your "belief thermostat." As Brian Tracy said, "you are a living magnet. What you attract into your life is in harmony with your dominant thoughts." Your thermostat is determined by your thoughts.

And the same applies for your performance in any area, whether it's weight control or goal achievement of any kind. You are either the *captain* or the *captive* of your thoughts. All of your abilities, feelings, behaviors, and actions are consistent with your self-image. ALWAYS.

If you rely upon your willpower or conscious efforts, the results will not be long lasting. You will always go back to that self-image, whether you're conscious of that image or not, just like a rubber band snaps back after you pull on it. You cannot escape your self-image! We always act and perform in accordance with what we imagine to be true about ourselves and our environment.

Your self-image is the result of deeply hidden and ingrained patterns of thought that you have held for years, possibly even decades. As Richard Bach notably stated, "argue for your limitations, and sure enough, they're yours." If these patterns of thought are altered, immediate changes and results can be achieved.

The good news is that your self-image and your thoughts CAN be changed!

Attitude is the answer. Your attitude toward your dreams

and goals either unlocks or locks the door to your success. When what you think, what you do, and how you feel are consistent, you are a winner. When those thoughts are positive and laser focused on what you want, you can achieve anything! Setting goals and having a positive attitude go hand in hand. Have the right attitude, and your goals will be much easier to accomplish. Believe that you can reach your goals, and you have VASTLY improved your chances of actually accomplishing those goals.

Try an exercise for three weeks if you want to change your income, for example. Give yourself three weeks of positive self-talk for self-worth and financial worth. Then, after the three weeks, set your goals and formulate a plan. When you determine who you really are on the inside, and what you are really capable of accomplishing, it is much easier to set goals and see the necessary steps to get from where you are to where you want to be.

Imagine setting your goals and having the fuel of positive self-talk and self-belief to back those goals up. You might achieve the goals without that great support, but you'd probably have a much more difficult time accomplishing them. Set your goals, work everyday at achieving them, and talk to yourself in positive ways along the way, every step of the way. By having a firm inner foundation, supported by a positive self-image and self-esteem, you will grant your journey the assurance of a safe arrival.

I talked earlier about what I consider the two main causes of procrastination and one of those is "belief." It's rare that we will attempt to do something that we don't believe in, and we will never give 100% of our effort to something without a strong belief that we can do it. It's our human defense mechanism. **In *As a Man Thinketh*, James Allen tells us, "The will to do springs from the knowledge that we can do." In *Above Life's Turmoil* he tells us, "Belief always precedes action."**

Our limiting beliefs are created and sustained by our limiting thoughts (some of which we inherited from others), our limiting words (some of which we inherited from others) and the limiting people in our life. Changing our limiting beliefs is such an important part of success that we spend a lot of time and put a lot of emphasis on it when we're working with our Champions Club. To a person I believe they would all agree that their work on their limiting beliefs has yielded the greatest results. It's allowed some of them to start their own business, triple their income and reach goals in half the time they thought it would take.

How powerful are your beliefs? Dr. Maxwell Maltz, the legendary author of *Psycho-Cybernetics* said, **"Within you right now is the power to do things you never dreamed possible. This power becomes available to you just as soon as you can change your beliefs."** A human being can create ANYTHING he can imagine. We wouldn't be able to imagine it otherwise!

Constantly ask yourself if your thoughts are helping you or hurting you. Are they getting you closer to or further away from where you want to be? Are they motivating you to action, or taking you further away due to fear and self-doubt? Learn to look for and focus on the positive. It will be a critical component in your creating the life that you want.

The following poem is by W.D. Windle, and it describes

the power of belief perfectly:

> If you think you are beaten, you are.
> If you think you dare not, you don't.
> If you like to win, but you think you can't,
> It is almost certain you won't.

> If you think you'll lose, you're lost,
> For out of the world we find,
> Success begins with a fellow's will—
> It's all in the state of mind.

> If you think you are outclassed, you are,
> You've got to think high to rise,
> You've got to be sure of yourself before
> You can ever win a prize.

> Life's battles don't always go
> To the stronger or faster man,
> But soon or late the man who wins
> Is the man who thinks he can!

Focus on reasons why you *can* achieve your goal rather than reasons why you cannot. Focus on solutions rather than excuses. There are always obstacles standing between where we are and where we want to be. Focus on the destination and the obstacles will vanish.

NOW IT'S TIME TO TAKE ACTION:

Exercise 1: Both our behaviors and our feelings are a result of our beliefs. To root out the belief that is responsible for your feelings and behaviors, ask yourself some questions.

Is there something you would like to accomplish, but you feel that you can't?

Once you identify the answer to that question, ask yourself why you feel you can't accomplish it. Why do you believe that you can't achieve it?

Is this belief based on actual facts, or is it based on a false assumption or conclusion? Is there any rational reason for such a belief? Could it be that you are mistaken about this belief?

What if someone you knew had this same belief?

If there is no seemingly good reason to continue to believe it, why should you continue to act and feel as if it were true?

Really contemplate and think about these questions. Think hard on them. Get emotionally involved in this process!

Can you see how you have continually sold yourself short, all based on beliefs that you thought were true, and yet were merely an illusion?

Have a real heart-to-heart talk with yourself. Honestly assess whether you have any problems that you have accepted as fact, and thus have finished working towards improving them.

Once you have identified those problems, apply rational thought to challenge these deeply held beliefs. Use your imagination to try out some new and different possibilities. Ask yourself the following questions:

Why do I believe that I can't?

IS there really a rational reason to believe such a thing?

COULD I be mistaken in regards to this belief?

What if a loved one had this belief? Would I support them, and allow them to keep believing such a thing, or would I want them to change it for their own benefit?

If there is no good reason to continue believing this, why should I continue to act and behave as though it were true?

What is a new, empowering belief that I can use to replace this limiting belief?

• • •

Exercise 2: Once you have identified your limiting beliefs, set aside time when you can turn outside distractions off and get quiet inside. Write out the top 5-10 limiting beliefs you can identify that are holding you back. Things like "I don't have enough time," "I always have such a hard time _____ (fill in the blank)," and "I can't ever seem to get ahead," are just a few examples of limiting beliefs.

Take each limiting belief you've written down and research and find the evidence that the belief is not true. That was one of the keys to Roger Bannister's success and my own as well. I like to find examples of others who have my circumstances that have succeeded in spite of their circumstances.

I suggest you rent (or better yet buy) the movie "Rudy." It's one of the most incredible examples of the power of belief that I've ever seen. I've seen the movie so many times I quit counting at 25.

• • •

Exercise 3: One of the most common goals relates to

something that almost everyone wants more of: MONEY. The common belief related to money is that we must work harder and longer in order to get more money. However, this is just a belief. IT'S NOT FACT. Your belief about money is either helping you or hurting you from getting more of it. T. Harv Ecker states that "there is a secret psychology to money. Most people don't know about it. That's why most people never become financially successful. A lack of money is not the problem; it is merely a symptom of what's going on inside you." A lack of money is a direct result of our limiting beliefs. The present state of your bank account and net worth is simply a physical manifestation of your previous thinking. You must change your thoughts and beliefs regarding money IMMEDIATELY in order to create more financial wealth in your life.

In order to become wealthy and earn more money, you need to recognize, identify, root out, and replace any negative or limiting beliefs you have regarding money. Some common beliefs are that money doesn't grow on trees, you have to work harder to make more, there's not enough money to go around, you're not spiritual if you're rich, etc.

Here are three steps to turn around your limiting beliefs regarding money:

1. Write down your limiting belief.

2. Challenge that belief. Argue with it. What are some reasons why the statement isn't true? List examples proving the falseness of the statement.

3. Create a positive statement that is the direct opposite of that negative statement. Repeat this statement throughout the day, until it becomes a reality.

Secret #5:
Stand on the Shoulders of Giants

WORLD-CLASS ACHIEVERS **never waste valuable time re-inventing the wheel. While some of them appear to be master innovators, they are in fact masters at studying previous successes and applying a new angle or new twist to an old idea.**

I always have the same advice for anyone who is about to embark on a goal that may be radically new to them. And it's wisdom that's at least as old as the Greeks. It's the shortest route to success: find someone who's doing what you want to do (or has the results you want to achieve). Study and determine what they did to achieve their result. Then simply engage in the same activities that brought them success and you'll be on a collision course with your goal.

I jokingly (but truthfully) tell audiences that I don't do anything original. Everything I do is something I copied from somebody else. But I also tell them my biggest secret—**I always copy from the very best**.

It's easy to trace this principle in areas like music. 1950's idol Buddy Holly copied some of the style and music of legendary bluesman Muddy Waters, who had copied from the icon Robert Johnson. Later, the Rolling Stones copied some of the style and music of Holly (and Waters and Johnson). AC/DC copied some of the style and music of the Stones, and the list goes on and on, always moving forward with a slightly different twist to an old idea.

I'm not sure why neophytes will many times want to re-invent the wheel. I don't know whether it's a fragile ego screaming for satisfaction, or whether it's remembering our days in school when copying from someone else was frowned upon (and has been cause for dismissal of many a promising student). But I do know this, **if you want to spend more time, more money and endure more frustration than you would otherwise, then strike out on an unproven path to your goal.**

On the other hand, if you're looking to significantly improve your odds of success and get to your goal on the straightest, shortest path, find someone you can model.

NOW IT'S TIME TO TAKE ACTION:

Take the biggest goal you have that you've been struggling with and find someone (Internet research has made this so easy) who's achieved it or something similar. Begin a study of them and their methods. If possible, figure out a way to meet them and get around them. Look for the things they did that you can copy. How can you apply your skill or your particular perspective to what they did? How can you make it "new," "improved" or "different"?

THEY ARE PROBABLY THE TWO biggest problems I consistently hear from those that we coach and consult: "I can't seem to stay focused," and "I never seem to find the time during the day to work on my goals."

We lay out some great goals, maybe even writing them down like the experts encourage. We enthusiastically start taking action. We can feel the power and the energy. We know that this time we're on the right track, this time is going to be different than all those other times.

Then it happens...

Life gets in the way!

Maybe it's a personal or family illness; or things get turned upside down at work. Maybe an unexpected financial crisis occurs. Whatever the interruption, it consumes us and before we know it, our once bright and shining goal that was out there in front of us is now just a tarnished and painful memory of what we could do if such and such hadn't happened.

Life gets in the way of everybody, but the more successful have a way of keeping their focus in spite of life. Whether it's watching a master like Peyton Manning leading his team to a fourth quarter comeback or a third-grader playing a brand new video game, it's obvious that Champions know how to concentrate their energy and efforts on what they want and blocking out anything or anyone who threatens that focus.

In ***As A Man Thinketh***, James Allen writes, "Having conceived of his purpose, a person should mentally mark out a straight pathway to its achievement, looking neither to the right nor left." With that in mind, stop and think about the analogy of planning a trip by car. Typically you'd select a route on the map that got you to your destination as quickly as possible. If you didn't need to reach your destination by a certain time, you might take detours along the route to see or do other things of interest to you. If it wasn't important that you reached your destination, you might choose to end your trip on one of your detours and never make it to the intended destination.

I see many comparisons to that analogy when I'm investigating a "lack of focus" with some of our clients. After a lot of probing we are able to determine that the destination (the goal) really isn't as important in the final analysis as they originally thought it was. Remember in Secret # 2 I talked about the power of Desire. How important it was to have a desire for our goal that is *consuming, obsessive, pulsating and burning*.

If you are having a problem staying focused, the first place to look is at the goal.

> **Is it really *my* goal – or is it someone else's goal for me?**

➡ **Why is the goal important to me?**

➡ **Is it a big enough "why" (see Secret #1)?**

➡ **How will I feel if I don't achieve the goal?**

Your answers to those questions may indicate whether you're ever likely to develop a Champion's focus on that goal.

E.L. Doctorow said that "most people are quiet in the world, and live in it tentatively, as if it were not their own." When you allow others to make your goals for you, or when you just allow life to happen to you, you aren't taking conscious control over your situations and circumstances. You are escaping into the vague and indefinable, rather than confronting the specific and measurable.

Perhaps you spend too much of your time NOT focused on your goals and dreams. Some people let any outside distraction deter them from focusing on what they want. They listen and pay attention to television, radio, newspapers and advertisements, even overheard conversations. They forget how to dream and they forget what it is that they want out of life. Don't fall into this trap. Be conscious of how you spend your time. Are you choosing how to spend your time, or are you letting other people choose for you?

Perhaps there are too many things that you wish to do. If you're very successful you're never going to have enough time to do everything you WANT to do. There are simply too many opportunities available to you everyday. In fact, if anything, World-Class Achievers have more challenges managing time because of the abundance they attract.

You may not have time to do everything you WANT to do, but when you're focused you'll have plenty of time to do everything you NEED to do to reach your goal. Goal setting is really nothing more than deciding in advance how you will allocate your time, talent and treasure in order to achieve a pre-determined objective. When you're focused on the goal, you are more likely to stick to your original allocation plan.

James Allen also told us that all successful people "hold fast to an idea, a project, a plan, and will not let it go; they cherish it, brood upon it, tend and develop it; and when assailed by difficulties, they refuse to be beguiled into surrender; indeed, the intensity of the purpose increases with the growing magnitude of the obstacles encountered." And that last sentence is the true secret: "indeed, the intensity of the purpose increases with the growing magnitude of the obstacles encountered."

It's not enough to simply say, "My goal is to be happy, " or to say, "I want to be healthy," or "I want to be wealthy." The mind and the Universe respond more quickly and positively when your goals and desires are specific.

Perhaps your goals aren't specific enough. Can you really laser in on your goals? Can you REALLY see them in your mind's eye? If you can't see them clearly, it always helps to write them down.

Another major problem that people face is the dreaded five syllable word:

Procrastination.

Procrastination is one of the biggest time and dream stealers. All of us have procrastinated during our lifetime, some of us more than others. Procrastination is a choice between one action and another. Procrastination itself doesn't make you a failure or a success; you simply made a choice between an action that will bring success, and an action that will bring failure.

Luckily, there are some techniques that can help you to push through the bad habit of procrastination.

In his audio program "Mind For Success Brain Series,"

Doug Bench mentions some exercises to help you push through procrastination. He calls these exercises "Newton's Law" and "The Final Four."

"The Final Four" is a fun and easy exercise you can use to help you get started on your daily tasks. Before doing this exercise, actually commit that you will begin to perform these tasks! The earlier in the day you do this exercise, the better. Don't wait until you're about ready to go to bed for the night!

Take a sheet of paper and list the tasks you need to get done that day. List them one by one, one under another, going down the sheet of paper. Once you list all of the tasks, go back to the top of the page.

Put brackets connecting the first two items. Put brackets connecting the new two items. Keep going down the page until all of the tasks have brackets connecting them, two tasks at a time. Go back to the first two tasks. Ask yourself which task is the easiest of the two tasks. Write the easier task to the right of the bracket. Do this for your whole list. Keep making brackets and choosing the easier task. Eventually you will end with one task. This task should be the easiest task of your whole list. Complete this task FIRST.

"Newton's Law" refers to Newton's Law of Motion. This law states that a body at rest tends to stay at rest, and a body in motion tends to stay in motion. Many people say to start with your most difficult task first and get it out of the way. However, this goes against Newton's Law of Motion.

Complete "The Final Four" exercise, and begin with the easiest task on the list. When you begin with the easiest task, as opposed to the hardest or most important task, you are more likely to complete other tasks on your list. You will generate momentum and carry this energy throughout your day.

When you solve the focus dilemma, you'll also solve most of your biggest struggles with managing time.

NOW IT'S TIME TO TAKE ACTION:

Take a lesson from expert marksmen who get totally focused on their target. Starting tonight before you retire take an index card and write down the most important goal in your life today. Flip over the index card and write down the number one activity you need to do to get you one step closer to the goal. Meditate on both sides thoroughly just before you go to bed and then discard it from your mind (let your subconscious work on it while you sleep). Upon arising spend some time again meditating on both sides. After your work day has begun attempt to complete the activity before you do anything else. If it's an activity that can only be done later in the day, keep reviewing both sides of the card during your breaks, lunch, etc. until you've completed the activity. Do the same thing every evening for a week. If you still haven't taken any action on the goal, then it's time to go back and read Secret # 1.

Secret #7:
Act Now, and Keep Acting

IN THE CHRISTIAN BIBLE one of the writers gives us the following wisdom: "Faith without works is dead."

World-Class Achievers know if you don't take action on a dream or a goal it will eventually die. They also know that taking action now, being decisive, is simply a habit that can be learned. The great success icon Lee Iacocca said that, "if I had to sum up in one word what makes a good manager, I'd say decisiveness. You can use the fanciest computers to gather the numbers, but in the end you have to set a timetable and act."

The rewards we receive in life come as a result not of your potential, but rather are a result of your performance.

It's been said that, "the masses make decisions slowly and change them quickly" while the super-successful "make decisions quickly and change them slowly, if at all." **World-Class Achievers don't wait until they have ALL the information before they decide to do something. They know it's only important to have ENOUGH information to make a decision.** Since they fully embrace failure (I'll tell you about that in Secret # 9) they don't let fear stop them from taking action on their decision.

I have often been amazed at how little action I have to take on a big decision before some great things start to happen. It's almost as if the energy of my action attracts many times that amount of energy from the universe. If nothing else, taking fast and decisive action gives me confidence and energizes me because I have overcome the natural inertia of my lower self.

One sound idea coupled with some action is all one needs to achieve success. Getting into action increases the likelihood of maintaining action. And that's supported scientifically by Newton's Law of Motion: "A body at rest tends to remain at rest and a body in motion tends to remain in motion." It is the continuing motion that creates momentum, or as it's fondly called, the "Big Mo."

We know "momentum" to be a cornerstone concept of physics. And while I don't understand physics, I know that when I climb on a bicycle, I can expect the first few turns of the pedal to require some significant effort to get me moving. I also know that I can use a short burst of intense energy to pedal the bicycle up to speed, and once up to speed, I can relax some as I pedal only enough to maintain the speed or momentum.

The bottom line: it's harder to get into action than it is to stay in action. So just get started! All that you need will come to you—when you are ready for it. Merely wishing for a thing does NOT mean that you are ready to receive it. It is your conscious mind's job to pay strict attention to its current task, to whatever you are doing, and to whatever is going on around you. You are able to act and react accordingly to what happens around you.

However, it is NOT your conscious mind's job to complete the task for you! You cannot force it to work in a way that it is not meant to work. You can't expect more out of it than it is even capable of doing. This process of achieving goals doesn't always work in a conscious way. We're not always aware of the progress we're making. But the creative mechanism works unconsciously. We're not supposed to see it working!

There is no given guarantee that we will receive what we want. We don't know what is taking place beneath the surface. This process requires trust, belief, and FAITH. And only by trusting and believing do we receive unforeseen signs and wonders.

In *Psycho-Cybernetics*, Maxwell Maltz makes the reader aware of the five laws that govern the operation of a successful human life. Knowing these five mental laws will help you to control your behavior in a positive way. Understanding these laws will help you to understand the cause of your results, and will help you to change those results for the better.

The first mental law is the **law of cause and effect**. This law states that for every action or event in your life, there is first a prior cause. Every effect in your life is due to a prior cause. Your manner of thinking will always be the primary cause for the results you are experiencing in your life. If you want to change your life, your thinking MUST change.

The second mental law is the **law of control**. This law states that you must accept responsibility for a situation before you can change it. Once you take responsibility for your life, you can take active control over your life circumstances. You must accept responsibility for your thoughts, feelings, and actions before you can begin to change them for the better.

The third mental law is the **law of belief**. Your reality is based on your current beliefs. Every belief is a choice. They're not set in stone. You weren't born with them. Beliefs are the most powerful creative force in affecting positive change. Your brain's thoughts and commands are based on your beliefs. Your beliefs are completely in your own control.

The fourth mental law is the **law of concentration**. Whatever you concentrate on gains more focus in your experience. What you concentrate on is completely in your control. Whether you have a success-oriented consciousness or a failure-oriented consciousness is determined by what you willfully concentrate on. You must first create mentally what you want to create physically. What you choose to concentrate on determines what you manifest physically.

The fifth mental law is the **law of attraction.** You literally attract into your life whatever grows into your consciousness. You ALWAYS attract the people and circumstances that harmonize with your current vibration, set forth by your dominant thoughts.

Knowing, understanding, and applying these five mental laws to your advantage will greatly increase your success rate.

We must allow the results to take care of themselves. When we try to force the process and try to force things to happen before their gestation period is complete, we become stressed, worried, frustrated, and likely to give up. You can relieve stress and worry by allowing your subconscious, your creative mechanism, to work on your goals and desires. Trust this creative process; it's how your subconscious truly works best!

Researchers studying the brains of creative people have found a direct link between creativity and positive thinking. Positive people naturally consider a wide range of possibilities and options when achieving a particular goal. A positive attitude will inherently imply confidence in other abilities and possibilities. A positive thinker finds reasons why an idea WILL work, versus a negative thinker who focuses on why the same idea might not work.

We all possess the ability to enhance our creativity. Maltz identified four ways to free and use our inner creative mechanism:

1. Once you make a decision, don't second guess it. Focus on supporting your decision. Strive for the ability to make a good and solid decision. A simple way to do this is to choose what to eat at a restaurant, or what movie to see, and not second guess it. Don't ask someone else for their opinion. Making your own decision will send a strong message to your subconscious that you are a person that makes a firm decision and doesn't worry about the decision once it's been made.

2. Spend time thinking about your future, about future goals and tasks to accomplish. This is an important part of goal setting and of living a meaningful life. But the subconscious works best when it is focused on the present moment. Give time to dream development, but don't spend ALL of your time thinking about the future. Set aside specific times to think about the future, but allow ONLY that time. The rest of the time, practice the habit of giving all of your conscious attention to the present moment. Your creative mechanism only functions in the present time. Don't worry about future events. Don't worry about how you will react to an unforeseen circumstance or event. Allow yourself

to enjoy the present moment. Your subconscious will thank you for it!

3. An all too common cause of confusion, worry, and anxiety is the well known habit of trying to accomplish too many things at once. Frustration and tension are inevitable because we are trying to do the impossible. We think about what we SHOULD be doing, or we think about all of the other things to come on our long to do list. The truth is, despite our best efforts, we are only capable of doing one thing at a time! Once you accept this, once you REALLY accept it, you will notice stress and tension begin to melt away. Allow yourself to completely focus on the task at hand. You will be more relaxed and your subconscious will be able to work more effectively.

4. Solving problems can be done at the conscious level. But sometimes, the more we think about a current issue, the more frustrated we become at the apparent lack of a solution. Use the inner resource of your creative mechanism. Allow yourself to dismiss the issue from your mind, and "sleep on it." Your creative mechanism works best when it is left alone and is allowed to do its work. In sleep, there is no conscious input blocking it. This is why some of our best ideas surface when we are sleeping or in the shower. We are relaxed, and there is less conscious input coming into our minds. Allow your subconscious mind to surprise you with the answers!

Abraham Lincoln said it well: "Determine that the thing can and shall be done, and then we shall find the way."

General George S. Patton said, "Never tell people how to do things. Tell them what to do and they will surprise you with their ingenuity."

These two quotes can be applied to your relationship with your subconscious. Tell it what you want, and then simply allow it to help you get what you want!

Once you BELIEVE you can acquire what you desire, THEN you are ready for it. Open-mindedness and belief are essential requirements for readiness. When one is truly ready for something, it puts in its appearance. So keep dreaming and believing—soon you will be ready to receive!

The author and one of the stars of *The Secret*, Bob Proctor, emphasizes the importance of taking action: "No amount of reading or memorizing will make you successful in life. It is the understanding and application of wise thought which counts."

The time to act on an idea is at the time of its birth. So ACT upon an idea immediately! You'll be glad that you did.

NOW IT'S TIME TO TAKE ACTION:

Take one major goal or activity you've been putting off because you didn't want to deal with it. Things like filing your past due taxes, getting a physical or dental work or even cleaning out the garage. Choose some type of reward that you'll treat yourself to when you've reached the goal (make sure the reward is in proportion to the achievement). Make the decision—right now—that you will take some type of action on the goal in the next 24 hours. Then act—the confidence you gain, not to mention the burden that will be lifted, will inspire you to apply the principle to other goals in your life.

The Incubator Method:

Maxwell Maltz describes this method for generating new ideas in ***Psycho-Cybernetics***. Identify a particular problem or question for which you need clarity. Write the problem down just before retiring for the night, and then go to sleep, possessing full trust that you will come up with a solution to the problem. Confidently assign the problem to your subconscious mind, and expect to receive the answer during the night or upon waking in the morning. Place a pad of paper and a pen next to your bed. When an answer comes to you out of nowhere, write the idea down onto the pad of paper immediately. Otherwise, you will most likely fall back asleep and lose the idea. The average time of a thought's life in the conscious brain is 37 seconds. By writing it down, you help to place the idea into your long-term memory, and you will be more able to recall the idea later.

Mind-Mapping Method:

This is another idea presented by Maltz. This technique involves forming a "decision tree" of new ideas. Take a piece of paper, and in the middle write the main subject or topic for which you need some ideas. Draw a circle around the idea, and place several spokes/branches drawn out from the center. Write down your initial thoughts and ideas, one per branch. As a new idea comes from that idea, draw out another branch, and so on, one idea and thought per branch. To REALLY make it effective, and to REALLY spark your creative juices, use different color pens or markers for each idea. You'll end up with numerous branches, all of which will help you to solve your chosen problem.

I'VE HEARD IT SAID THAT we're born with only a few fears – like the fear of falling and the fear of loud noises. All other fears we learn along the way. Like the fear of failure, the fear of rejection - even a fear of success. I believe our greatest enemy in life is fear, because fear keeps us from doing many of those things we would like to do that would make our life more complete and more enjoyable.

Doubt is the first cousin of fear and precedes it. We weren't born with doubt. Our habit of doubt has grown throughout our life. If we dwell on a doubt and give in to it, it then grows into fear. In his epistle, the ancient writer James reminds us that doubt makes us ineffective, "a doubtful mind will be as unsettled as the wave of the sea that is tossed and driven by the wind; and every decision you then make will be uncertain, as you turn first this way, and then that."

Faith and fear are totally opposite views of the future. And because they are, they cannot co-exist. I once heard Zig Ziglar quote Mark Twain when he said, "True courage is not the absence of fear, it's the mastery of fear." World-Class Achievers have just as many fears as those who live miserable, unfulfilled lives because of fear—they have just learned to master their fears instead of allowing their fears to master them. In fact, because they play on a much larger stage, they have to confront the fear of things much larger than the masses will ever confront.

Along with fear and doubt, people commonly experience stress, sometimes repeatedly, on a daily basis. The problem is that stress is our body and brain's enemy! Up to 70% of all illness is related to stress. Stress releases toxins into our bodies, and physically creates illnesses. Stress also makes you more forgetful because thought impulses are stopped. They're not allowed to go from short-term to long-term memory.

Perhaps if we knew more about stress and its causes, we would be able to significantly reduce it or even eliminate its occurrence. Stress is simply negative visualizations! Practice your positive visualization techniques, and you will take control over your stress and over your life. If you have to, fake it! Act how a calm and stress-free person would act. Stop those negative thoughts from firing! Force yourself to be an actor, a relaxed and calm person, and you will become an achiever. Eliminate stress and you will eliminate 70% of pain's cause.

Negative emotions are alarms! The following emotions, as identified and explained in ***Psycho-Cybernetics***, will impede your success, IF you choose to focus on them:

Negative Emotions to Avoid at all Costs
Frustration
Aggressiveness
Hopelessness
Anger
Insecurity
Loneliness
Uncertainty
Emptiness
Resentment

Frustration develops whenever a goal we want to reach isn't yet realized. This negative emotion also develops when a strong desire is unfulfilled. If you experience chronic frustration, reexamine the goals you have set for yourself. Chances are, either the goal is unattainable at this point in time, or your image of you achieving this goal is not sufficient. Perhaps you're even suffering from both of these problems.

Insecurity results from feelings that we must be perfect at all times and at all costs. An insecure person believes they must always be happy, successful, and poised. These are all worthy goals to aim for, but they cannot be experienced ALL of the time.

Loneliness is a natural feeling for all of us to experience, at one time or another. However, chronic feelings of loneliness are signals to our brains and to the Universe that we are focused on lack and failure. We feel alienated from life and separate from the world around us.

Uncertainty can stop you dead in your tracks if you allow it to. It is a way of avoiding mistakes and responsibility. Uncertainty is based on the mistaken assumption that if no decision is made, nothing will go wrong. To the person who is afraid of making a mistake, decision-making becomes literally a life or death matter.

Emptiness is a feeling that results when you feel as though your achievements have been in vain. Along the way, you forgot that the whole point of setting and achieving goals is to ENJOY life. Those who forgot to have fun along the way ultimately end up feeling as though their time and efforts were a waste. When this occurs, no amount of wealth or achievement can bring personal success or happiness. Feeling emptiness in life is a symptom of not living creatively.

Suffering from a poor or inadequate self-image can cause feelings of emptiness as well. If you achieve your goals, but feel as though you don't deserve them, your achievements will feel empty and inconsistent with your self-image.

Comparing your successes and achievements to the achievements of others can result in feelings of resentment. You feel as though you are being short-changed in life, being given an unfair shot, and not earning the things you truly deserve. You use resentment as a means of justifying your failures. You begin to see yourself as a victim. You begin to use feelings of resentment as a means of feeling important.

These negative moods not only affect us, but also those around us, even the people we love the very most. Irritability, rudeness, gossip, and violence emerge through our continual negative thinking. If you understand your negative emotions, you can stop the thoughts causing the feelings and use that mental energy in a more productive and beneficial manner.

These emotions are inconsistent with creative goal achievement. When you are feeling these negative emotions, you become a passive creator of your life. You're no longer in control; instead, your circumstances are.

A negative thought or feeling is NOT eradicated by conscious effort or willpower. A bad feeling can only be displaced by a positive feeling. If you are feeling an undesirable emotion, don't concentrate on that unwanted emotion. Instead, immediately concentrate on positive and favorable images.

These images, when focused upon for a long enough period of time, will manifest positive, favorable feelings. The negative feeling will evaporate. Stay focused on positive images, and positive feelings will follow.

Despite our best intentions to feel positive, it's easy for us to feel fear and doubt. Why is this natural tendency so true? We're battling our own evolution! We have a mechanism in our brain whose main function is to keep us safe. The Amygdala keeps you safe by working endlessly to keep you THE SAME.

Back in the days of early human times, those who didn't face danger tended to live, while those who faced the dangers of predators and the outside world were more than likely killed. Those that thought the worst, that were fearful of the outside world, were the most likely to survive. This Amygdala is still part of our evolution! It is your friend in keeping you safe, but it is your mortal enemy when it comes to achievement!

When you start to change, the Amygdala releases chemical impulses to return you to where you were before. It AUTOMATICALLY fires negative thoughts. About 80% of our conscious thoughts are negative! You don't even have to be aware this is happening, it all happens at the subconscious level. Willpower and desire make no difference to the Amygdala! It will do whatever it takes to keep you the same, under the mistaken belief that change will be HARMFUL to you. Anxiety, discomfort, and stress naturally begin to appear when you are challenging your own comfort zone.

We are already equipped with these negativity indicators. They are our brain's means of communicating to us the possibility of danger. Even cars come equipped with negative performance indicators! To ignore negative signals, such as an empty gas tank or a failing engine, would ultimately result in your car becoming ruined and ineffective.

However, if you continually focus on these signals, you will hesitate on taking any sort of action to correct the problem. You must take positive actions to correct the problem! A red light on your dashboard doesn't mean that the car itself is defective. It simply means that some corrective action is needed. Once the action is taken, the car goes back to its optimum level of performance.

As you can see, you're up against a lot of negative indicators! How do you combat this natural part of your evolution? You continually, EVERY DAY, step outside of your comfort zone. If you want to change and grow, you MUST do things that are not natural for you to do. Get comfortable being uncomfortable! Get excited when you feel uncomfortable and anxious! It means that your Amygdala has recognized you're outside of your comfort zone. It means you're in the process of growing!

However, if this discomfort isn't recognized by you as a step outside of your comfort zone, these feelings can quickly spread like a virus into FEAR. High levels of fear stop the flow of thought impulses. You will become frozen and incapable of completing the task at hand. This is similar to the "deer in the headlights" expression. A deer is so filled with fear when approached by a car's shining headlights when it's in darkness, it literally freezes in its tracks. Its thoughts stop, and it is unable to move.

Statistically and scientifically, 97% of the things we worry about never occur! And guess what worry is caused by? The Amygdala! It's in our evolution to do this! HOWEVER, it's only a defect if you don't change it! Fight back against your evolution. Intercept negative images, thoughts, and visualizations so that they can't be completed. Jump in front of it, stop it, and turn it into a positive.

The Amygdala automatically fires chemicals that will try to keep you from taking action. You can't control it consciously. Your conscious thoughts aren't even connected to the Amygdala, it doesn't even hear them! You MUST recognize discomfort as a step outside of your comfort zone, and take control of your thoughts AFTER the discomfort arises. Don't allow the discomfort and anxiety to grow into fear!

Almost all of your thought is done by habit at the subconscious level. It's a result of thinking in a habitual way. You MUST recognize your negative thoughts and create a new habit of thinking in a more positive and productive way.

In his book ***Change Your Brain, Change Your Life***, Dr. Daniel Amen refers to these negative thoughts as ANTs, or Automatic Negative Thoughts. He notes nine different ways that our thoughts lie to us to make our situation seem worse than it really is, and how we can change them for the better:

1. Always/Never Thinking

This type of thinking occurs when you think something that happened will "always" repeat itself in the future, or that you'll "never" get what you want. Some examples of this type of thinking are "this never works out," "no one ever calls me," and "he never listens to me." This type of thinking is so negative that it automatically makes you upset. If you find yourself thinking this way, stop and make yourself think of examples where the statement isn't true.

2. Focusing on the Negative

This type of thinking occurs when your thoughts reflect

only the bad in a situation. You ignore any of the good in a situation. Focusing only on negative situations will unnecessarily cause you to feel negativity. Look for the positive in a situation. Seeking the positive will bring you more balance and optimism.

3. Fortune telling

Fortune telling thinking causes you to predict the worst possible outcome to a situation. Predicting negative situations helps to make them happen. These thoughts pretty much kill your chances for feeling good. Instead, remind yourself that no one can accurately predict the future.

4. Mind Reading

Negative mind reading is when you believe you know what other people are thinking, even when they haven't told you what they're thinking. Some examples of this type of thinking are "she's mad at me," "he doesn't like me," etc. In reality, you can't read anyone's mind. When there's something you don't understand, ask the person for clarification.

5. Thinking with Your Feelings

When you believe your negative thinking without even questioning them, you are thinking with your feelings. You tell yourself, "I feel this way, so it must be true." "I feel like a failure." "I feel stupid." Feelings don't always tell the truth. Whenever you have a strong negative feeling, examine it. Look for what's causing the feeling. Are there real reasons to feel that way? Are your feelings based on things that happened in the past? Really examine what you're feeling to determine its validity.

6. Guilt Beating

Guilt isn't a helpful emotion, and it often causes you to

do things you don't want to do. "Should," "ought to," "must," and "have to" are all statements that are based out of guilt. Because of human nature, whenever we think we MUST do something, we automatically don't want to do it. You can replace guilt phrases with more helpful phrases, such as, "I want to," "It would be helpful to," and "I'm going to." Guilt is not productive. Get rid of guilt!

7. Labeling

Labeling occurs whenever you attach a negative label to yourself or someone else. You automatically stop your ability to take a clear look at a situation. Stay away from labels, such as "jerk," "lazy," and "irresponsible," both towards yourself and towards others.

8. Personalizing

Personalizing is when you attach two unrelated events with one another. An example of personalizing would be, "He didn't hug me this morning, he must be mad at me." Truth is, we never fully know why people do what they do. Try not to personalize the behaviors of others.

9. Blaming

Blaming is very harmful because when you blame someone or something else for your life, you become a passive victim to your circumstances. It becomes difficult to change your circumstances when you don't take full responsibility for them. "It wasn't my fault that…" and "He's responsible for…" are examples of blaming. Blaming hurts your personal sense of power. Before you can change your life, you must take full responsibility for your life.

If you want to change your habits, you must change your thoughts. It takes a MINIMUM of 21 days to form enough new thought connections in the brain to create a new habit. Once the task becomes a habit, your Amygdala will cease creating anxiety and discomfort. Your Amygdala will hibernate when you are performing this task. Successful people are constantly trying new things, even if they're tasks they aren't sure they know how to do. Avoid ANTs if you want to create new habits in order to change your life.

The more you feel uncomfortable in your goal achievement process, the more you will achieve! Make it a habit of getting outside of your comfort zone! Do something new on a daily basis. Constantly stretch your comfort zone. Even risk criticism and confrontation in order to seek new opportunities and ways of improving. You will be amazed at how quickly you will begin to achieve your goals.

Norman Vincent Peale, writing in **You Can If You Think You Can**, provides us with a prescription for mastering fear and doubt. "You can cancel out fear with faith. For there is no force in this world more powerful than faith. The most amazing things can happen as a result of it…There are two massive thought forces competing for control of the mind: fear and faith, and faith is stronger, much stronger. Hold that thought of faith's greater power until you believe it, for it can be the difference between success and failure."

The legendary golfer Jack Nicklaus personifies motivation backed by desire, rather than backed by fear. His mind only allows room for the task at hand, and never for any negative self-talk. He is a winner in life because of his amazing ability to focus on the present, and what is needed in the moment. He knows that when you believe, and concentrate on doing something well, your belief will grow and multiply. Opportunities will begin to take form and abound. He takes moments of risk and chooses to turn them into opportunities. Because he sees success in his mind, he is able to ignore the possibility of failure. He consciously forgets his past failures by actively focusing on the task at hand and imagining exactly what he wants to occur.

It really helps to understand that fear is nothing more than your perception of a future occurrence. As I pointed out in Secret #4 about limiting beliefs, the perception may not be based on truth, and that's generally the case with fear. You may have seen or heard the expression that uses the acronym F.E.A.R. to make the point that fear is "false evidence appearing real."

For instance, if you've been thinking about starting your own business but have been stymied by fear, it's probably because of some perception that the business might fail and then what would you do? That thought leads to even bleaker thoughts that you might lose your home or your car. There's really no evidence that any of those events will occur. It is all in your perception. Is it any wonder then that you can never take the necessary steps to do what you've always wanted to do?

World-Class Achievers master fear and doubt by confronting it—facing it—and by applying knowledge to the situation. Fear and doubt are most often caused by ignorance or avoidance of the real facts or truth. In addition, they know that the old aphorism to "do the thing you fear and fear will disappear" is some very powerful wisdom. Doubters never win, and winners never doubt.

Feelings of doubt, fear, and stress are recorded in your

subconscious. The language of your subconscious is told through your body's feelings. Unfortunately, negative feelings, if allowed to persist for a long enough period of time, can manifest in the body as physical pain.

Do you or someone you know suffer from chronic physical pain? Over 50 million people in the United States alone suffer from chronic pain. Physical pain severely impedes on your brain's ability to function successfully and well. Chronic pain shrinks your brain matter and influences the firing of your brain cells. Believe it or not, pain is actually located in the BRAIN, and NOT in the body. The brain processes excessive and chronic stress in a way that is NOT beneficial to our health and well-being. Unmanaged and allowed to fester, chronic stress manifests in our bodies as ulcers, high blood pressure, addictions, and other debilitating diseases and conditions.

Have you ever known an amputee who suffered from phantom pain? An amputee can literally feel pain in the limb that they are physically missing. To solve this problem, scientists developed a mirror box that reflects the present limb in such a way as making two limbs appear. By using this mirror box for 15 minutes, 3 times a day, for 3-4 weeks, amputees can make the phantom pain disappear. The subject sits in front of the mirror box, reflecting their missing limb. The amputee performs exercises using their good limb, making it appear as though there are two limbs performing the exercises perfectly. The mirror tricks the subconscious into believing the limb IS still present.

The subconscious no longer sees a cause for the pain to exist. Three to four weeks later, the phantom pain disappears.

A control group of amputees performed the same exercises, for the same time duration, without the mirror. Three to four weeks later, the phantom pain still remained.

To reduce your pain, overwhelm your brain! If you overload or distract your brain with impulses, the pain will be reduced significantly. The brain can only focus on the present moment. Focus on other impulses while you're feeling physical pain. Trick your brain into believing the pain is gone, and the pain will go away!

Worry and belief are two sides of the same coin. It all depends on which side you choose to focus on. You can change your focus from the negative to the positive. When you worry, you are picturing an undesirable outcome to occur in the future. You use no effort or willpower. The image seems to manifest effortlessly and readily. You keep dwelling on the end result, the possibilities that might happen, even if you DON'T want them to occur. You keep playing with the idea that this outcome MIGHT happen.

Worry is nothing more than negative visualization. Remember, the subconscious takes everything you think as real. It is 5/6 of your brain's thinking power! Worrying gives meaning to your statements. This constant repetition, of constantly replaying what you DON'T want, makes the end result become more and more real and vivid in your mind's eye. Soon, you find yourself feeling the emotions that accompany worry—fear, anxiety, stress, and discouragement. These emotions are completely appropriate for what you have been imagining all along.

Your nervous system CANNOT tell the difference between real worry and failure and imagined worry and failure. If you imagine failure in enough vivid detail, your body projects these feelings into the physical. If these thoughts are continued, on a regular basis, illness and disease will naturally result.

Luckily, you can flip the coin to the other side. Change the undesirable end result to what you DO want to occur. Imagine this end result just as vividly as you did the previous end result, the less desirable one. Imagine it over and over, repeating it just as many times as you did with the previous image. View high achieving actions if you want to be a high achiever! When you start to have a negative visualization, immediately stop it, and turn it into a positive picture. The proper response to feelings and thoughts of worry is to totally ignore them! Don't listen to them. Instead, turn your thoughts towards what you DO want.

Soon, you will begin to generate positive emotions that easily and naturally accompany this new, improved image. You will begin to feel enthusiasm, cheerfulness, joy, excitement, and happiness. They will automatically be generated. Call up and evoke feelings of success.

If you want to have more control over your life, generate a positive attitude, for "the habit of being happy enables one to be freed, or largely freed, from the domination of outward conditions," according to Robert Louis Stevenson. When you feel confident and successful, you will act successfully.

You can begin to form the habit of reacting to threats and problems in a positive and aggressive way. Take active control over your life! Form the habit of staying focused on your goals, regardless of the circumstances that may arise. You can practice a positive and aggressive attitude both in real circumstances and in your imagination. Send a strong message to your subconscious that you manage fear and doubt willingly and effectively.

See yourself solving a problem or achieving a goal through positive actions and decisions. Turn a crisis into an action activator. Remain goal oriented. Keep your positive goal in mind. The crisis will act as a stimulus and will release additional energy and power to help you accomplish your goals. In many instances, an event that began as a crisis ends as an opportunity that progresses you that much closer towards your goal.

Happiness isn't something that just happens to you. It doesn't pick who is happy and who isn't (although it may seem like it sometimes!). Happiness is an action verb. It requires a conscious decision to be happy! If you continue to wait for happiness to come to you, to arrive at your doorstep, you will likely continue to wait for a long time. If you wait for your circumstances to improve, for your life to be ideal, before you can be happy, you are likely to wait forever.

We can make our own happiness, because we choose our own thoughts! We choose our own self-images! This is a good thing, because that means that happiness is entirely UP TO YOU.

It is your choice which side of the coin to focus on. Your subconscious can focus on either one. It is unable to question the data and information you program into it. It simply processes the information and reacts to it accordingly. It can operate as a failure mechanism or as a success mechanism. You can be happy or you can be sad. It all depends on the data you give it and the goals you set for it. Your subconscious is a goal-striving mechanism. It's completely up to you which one it functions as!

We think, feel, learn, and perform better when we are in a happy, pleasant state of mind. Even our physical body works better when we are in a positive state of mind. Our stomach, heart, liver, and all of our internal organs function more optimally when we are happy. Many scientific studies have been conducted, and time and time again, they prove that a pleasant state of mind helps bring about a better performing body. Russian psychologist K. Kekcheyev tested people when they were thinking pleasant and unpleasant thoughts. When people thought pleasant thoughts, their seeing, hearing, tasting, and touching senses were enhanced, versus when the subjects were thinking unpleasant thoughts.

Most people unconsciously and without awareness set up goals for failure. They continually hold negative images and fear of failure, and wonder why they aren't living the life they want to be living.

You, however, have been given the information and tools needed to separate yourself from this vast majority of failure-driven people. It's up to you which side of the fence you choose to live on. You can live a success driven life, or a failure driven life. Which one do you choose? I suggest the success driven life, it's much more fun and enjoyable!

In the final analysis, fear is present in everyone's life. In only creates a problem when it causes inaction and paralysis. Fear is never a reason for quitting. Quitting due to fear is merely an excuse. It's okay to be afraid, in fact, it's normal! Whenever you begin to feel fear, remind yourself of your desire to achieve your goals. Remember your why. Desire is the perfect antidote for fear and despair. Conquer fear and you truly have gained one of the real "keys to the kingdom."

If you don't feel like a winner, project the feeling as though you DO feel like a winner! Winners are walking examples of positive self-projection. You can always spot a winner from a mile away. They project an unmistakable and unforgettable aura and presence. First impressions are extremely powerful and create lasting impressions on the people around you. CHOOSE to project yourself as a winner, and soon you will BE a winner!

Reflect on the following poem by Henry Van Dyke, entitled "Thoughts Are Things," to remind you of our thoughts' vast power and importance:

> I hold it true that thoughts are things,
> They're endowed with bodies and breath and wings:
> And that we send them forth to fill
> The world with good results, or ill.
>
> That which we call our secret thought
> Speeds forth to Earth's remotest spot,
> Leaving its blessings or woes
> Like tracks behind as it goes.
>
> We build our future, thought by thought,
> For good or ill, yet know it not.
> Yet so the Universe was wrought.
> Thought is another name for fate;
> Choose then thy destiny and wait,
> For love brings love and hate brings hate.

NOW IT'S TIME TO TAKE ACTION:

Take one of your biggest fears and on a sheet of paper list the fear using as much detail as possible. For instance, if you have a fear of speaking in front of others, don't just say "Fear of speaking in front of others." Say "I have a fear of speaking in front of others because _____ _____(fill in the blank).

Once you've listed the fear, now list all of the possible outcomes if you were to take action in spite of the fear. For instance, what are all the things that could possibly happen if you got up and spoke to a group of people? One outcome is you could get a standing ovation. Another outcome is you could get polite applause. And certainly one possible outcome is that you could be booed. Be very thorough and list every one you can possibly think of.

Now go back and review each outcome and ask yourself two questions:

What's the worst thing that can happen to me if I had this outcome?

Could I carry on with my life if the very worst happened?

If you're truthful with yourself, it will be a very rare occurrence that you would find an outcome that would be so bad that you couldn't carry on.

Now, with your changed perception of the future, take some type of action step as you assure yourself that no matter what the outcome, you're going to make it.

• • •

Exercise 2: Kill Your Ants/Feed Your Anteater

This exercise is from Dr. Daniel Amen's book *Change Your Brain, Change Your Life*. Whenever you notice an ANT, or Automatic Negative Thought, you need to crush it, or it will take over your life in a negative way. Once you notice a negative thought and correct it, you immediately take away its power. If you allow a negative thought to go unnoticed or unchanged, your mind believes it and your body reacts to it.

ANTs are generally illogical, and yet we tend to believe them. By bringing them from a subconscious to a conscious level of awareness, we are able to see just how little sense they really make. To find out what's true and what isn't true in your life (i.e. "I am not creative"), you need to question your ANTs. Don't believe everything you hear, even in your own mind!

Ask yourself about your ANT population. Is it high, low, increasing, decreasing? Keep control over them. Whenever you recognize one entering your mind, train yourself to recognize it and write it down. Talk back to it! Gain back control from your negative thoughts.

Examples of ANTs

You never listen to me.

My boss hates me.

Everyone will laugh at me.

I'm stupid.

It's not my fault, it's his.

Once you've identified the ANT, counteract it with a positive statement. Kill the ANT!

He's listened to me before.

My boss could just be having a bad day.

Maybe everyone will like my speech.

I've made smart decisions in the past.

I can make the situation better. It's up to me.

Select a period of time, such as a day or a week, to monitor your ANTs. Carry paper and pen with you, and write one down when you identify it. Immediately write down a counter statement to that negative thought. This exercise is VERY powerful!

• • •

Exercise 3: This exercise, also suggested by Dr. Amen, is good for when you are feeling worry and anxiety over a situation:

1. Write down the event causing you anxiety or worry.
2. Notice and write down the automatic thoughts coming into your mind.
3. Label or identify the negative thoughts as a fortune telling ANT (when you focus only on the negative possibilities). Often just naming and labeling a thought can help to take away its power.
4. Talk back to the negative thought and kill it! Write down a positive response to kill the negative thought.

Remember, thoughts aren't always real. Choose to predict the best outcomes to your situations.

• • •

Exercise 4: This exercise is good during the moment you are feeling anxiety. Slight changes in the oxygen content in the brain alter the way a person feels and behaves. When a person is angry, their breathing pattern changes almost immediately. The breathing becomes faster and shallower. The oxygen content in the person's blood is lowered, and less oxygen is available to the brain. The person most likely becomes angry, confused, irritable, and prone to negative and impulsive behavior.

When you are feeling anxious or upset, consciously shift your breathing from your chest and breathe slowly and deeply from your belly. Kill the negative thoughts by distracting yourself from the anxiety.

The way you breathe has a huge impact on how you feel each moment. By shifting your breathing from your chest to your belly, you will feel more relaxed and in control of the situation.

Secret #9:
FIDO is More than a Dog's Name

ONE OF THE MOST INSPIRATIONAL people I've ever heard is a former Marine Lieutenant named Clebe McClary. Critically wounded in Vietnam, Clebe was presented the Silver Star and the Bronze Star by the President of the United States. And although he suffered the loss of an eye, an arm and then underwent 34 operations to retain usage of the remainder of his body, he never lost the determination, dedication and courage to overcome his circumstances.

I heard Clebe during the time in my life when I most needed to hear him because I had been "critically wounded" in my own special way. During the financial disaster I described in Secret #4, I heard Clebe describe the acronym that not only helped him get up out of the hospital bed but helped him create a remarkable life. **The acronym F.I.D.O. stands for "Forget it – Drive On!"**

Now isn't that just like a Marine.

I can't tell you how many times I've used that to move past a negative circumstance. To this day I will repeat to myself "Forget it –Drive On!" when any kind of disaster or distraction takes place.

Success breeds success. Winners forget past failures, and focus instead on past successes. Both are readily available, but which one you focus on is entirely up to your choosing.

One of the principal fears we have is the fear of failure.

Winners know that the number of times they've failed in the past doesn't matter. Each failure was a step towards their goals and achievements. They were a necessary part of the growth process. One of the most common causes of failure is the habit of quitting when one is temporarily overcome by defeat.

Failure is very tricky and cunning. It will do all it can to stop you in your tracks. It is almost always near when one is about to cross the finish line, about to achieve a long sought after goal. However, every failure brings with it the seed of an equal success. Successful people do not quit! Don't let temporary defeat stop you.

An early president of IBM, Thomas J. Watson, agreed with the importance of failing forward. He simply said, "Double your failure rate." Many people don't take action because they're afraid to fail. They think that successful people never make mistakes, and therefore they don't take action because they are not already successful. This is a common misconception.

Successful people know that failure is an essential part of the learning process. Failure allows us to learn through trial and error. Mistakes allow us to learn new information. You must be eager and willing to fail! Get started, make mistakes, learn from those mistakes, correct the mistakes, and keep moving forward towards your goal. Every tried experience will give you more information to help you proceed towards the next step on your journey.

In Doug Bench's "Mind Your Brain Success System" audio program, he says we should "be a baby" when we're learning or trying something new. Babies see other people walking and decide to follow in their footsteps. They attempt to follow their walking companions. They learn by failing, time and time again. The more they fall, the more new thought connections are formed. The brain works hard to find a solution that will allow them to walk. They fail, time and time again, and yet they enjoy every minute of it!"

We were all babies. We all experienced this walk and fail method. Ask your brain to help you learn from failure. Every time you fail, you make new connections in your brain by forcing your brain to change the thoughts that caused you to fail. Be a baby, and you will see your achievements rise to the top!

Bench also recommends that we fail at something daily, no matter how simple or complex the activity or experience was. He suggests to write down what you failed at and what you learned from that experience. This act will help to remind you of the importance of failure. It will send a strong message to your subconscious, saying it's okay to fail! The most successful people in today's world are those that fail, for failure is essential to success.

A portion of the brain is activated when you fail. The brain is consolidating that information and organizing it. It's finding out the reasons why you failed and how it can help prevent you from making that mistake in the future. You will be more likely to reach better results when you perform that activity in the future. Fail as fast as you can and as often as you can to achieve better results!

Your subconscious contains memories of all past failures and of all past painful and negative experiences. These negative experiences and failures actually HELP in the learning process, but ONLY if they are used effectively and properly. They are feedback to your subconscious and help your subconscious correct course towards the goal desired. Every memory in your brain is a perfect memory. You want to learn and experience all that you can. Your brain will have more information to draw upon in the future when you're trying to accomplish a goal or solve a problem.

When you accomplish anything new, something is occurring in your brain. When you make a mistake, your prefrontal cortex automatically and subconsciously searches for ways to give you an answer or solution. It draws upon past experiences and information.

However, this can work for you OR against you. If you imagine what you DON'T want, the subconscious takes the images as real. Your prefrontal cortex will form connections that indicate it's what you DO want. Go back to the "don't spill the milk" example. If you tell yourself not to spill milk, the subconscious takes the image as real. Your prefrontal cortex will work to help you spill the milk. What do you do? You spill the milk, despite your best conscious efforts to do otherwise.

Therefore, you want to concentrate on what you DO want to happen, especially after making a mistake. Take the game of golf for example. When you miss a putt, immediately afterwards concentrate in your mind's eye on making the putt. Maybe make an imaginary putt with your putter. That's what Phil Mickelson and other great golfers are doing when they miss that big putt.

Concentrate on what you do want to happen. This simple step will tell your prefrontal cortex what you want to occur, and it will go to work on helping you to make that desire happen.

Through repetition, you can develop new, more positive patterns of thought. Repeated enough times, these new patterns of thought become habitual. Creating and holding firmly in mind a positive image of what you desire is the key to eliminating unnecessary fear from your life.

Martial arts expert and movie star Bruce Lee had an exercise to rid himself of negative thoughts. He identified the negative thought, visualized writing it down on a piece of paper, crumpling up the paper, lighting it on fire, and allowing it to burn until it was just a pile of ashes. This exercise sends a strong message to your subconscious. It tells it to forget the negative thought and drive on regardless!

When an error has been made, and recognized as simply a deviation from the desired goal, the error MUST be consciously forgotten and put aside. The desired outcome MUST be remembered and dwelt upon. Your past failures will not harm your future successes, as long as you focus on the goal that you want to accomplish.

Attempting new things and allowing yourself the possibility of failure will automatically help you to stretch your comfort zone. Your comfort zone, although keeping you safe and comfortable, is a self-created prison. It consists of a lifelong collection of beliefs that have been accumulated and reinforced throughout your life.

However, you can expand your comfort zone. You can use affirmations and visualization to help you create in your mind what you want and actions you need to take. Then perform those actions! All of these approaches will help you to stretch your comfort zone and live the life you deserve to be living.

There is no such thing as being "stuck." When you feel

stuck, you are simply repeating the same thoughts and seeing the same images over and over again. You're not thinking new thoughts or seeing new things.

Decide to expand your comfort zone. Allow yourself to fail, if need be. You will be automatically expanding your comfort zone and allowing yourself to fail forward.

Einstein knew this fact when he stated, "the significant problems we face cannot be solved by the same level of thinking that created them." Stretch your comfort zone by flooding your subconscious with new thoughts and images. See your goals as already complete.

See the world as supporting you in accomplishing your goals and dreams. Use the same viewpoint as Stan Dale: "I've always been the opposite of a paranoid. I operate as if everyone is part of a plot to enhance my well-being."

W. Clement Stone was known as an inverse paranoid. He chose to believe that the world was plotting to do him well. He refused to believe that people were out to do him harm. He saw every difficulty and opportunity as a chance to become empowered, enriched, and advanced in his causes.

New experiences will always feel at least somewhat scary. They're supposed to, that's how they work! Every time you face a new experience, and follow through, you create that much more confidence in your abilities.

Each day, repeat the following phrase, as suggested by Jack Canfield in his book *The Success Principles*:

"I believe the world is plotting to do me good today. I can't wait to see what it is!"

All learning is a gradual process, and involves progressing through four levels of competence:

1. Unconscious incompetence: In this level, you are totally unaware that you even lack a certain skill or ability.

2. Conscious incompetence: In this level, you lack a particular skill or ability, but are aware that you lack this skill.

3. Conscious competence: In this level, you are able to perform a certain task or ability well, and you are aware of this fact.

4. Unconscious competence: In this final level of learning, you automatically perform a certain task well, and you never think about how to perform it. At this level, your behavior is habitual and carried out at the subconscious level.

An example of these stages of learning is driving a car. When we're babies, we are unconsciously incompetent. We're not even aware that we don't know how to drive a car.

At the conscious incompetent level, we become aware that we don't know how to drive a car.

At the conscious competent level, we become able to drive a car, but we still have to think about what we're doing. It's not yet second nature.

At the unconscious competent level, we're able to talk on the phone, eat a sandwich, read the paper, and drive the car at the same time. Don't try these things all at once, though!

You must recognize your errors and mistakes as necessary steps towards the fulfillment of your goals and desires. However, they must be forgotten and NOT dwelt upon. Dwelling upon them consciously, or feeling guilt about them, will cause us to continually relive the past, relive those things we do not want, but can't seem to escape from.

How many people do you know who constantly and endlessly talk about what they DON'T want, and yet continually find themselves experiencing those very things? Too many unfortunately. Continually dwelling on the past and on unwanted experiences only serves to bring them about more often and readily.

The minute we change our minds, and CHOOSE to stop focusing on and reliving the past, we will gain control over our future, and relinquish control over the past.

The vast majority of people are ready to throw in the towel upon ANY sign of temporary defeat or misfortune. The truly successful and outstanding achievers of this world continue on, despite their failures, no matter how numerous or plentiful. These people are the truly outstanding achievers of this world.

Walt Disney said his big growth came when he went from merely wishing to create Disney World to becoming DETERMINED to create the ultimate amusement park even though a group of amusement park owners criticized and laughed at his ideas. Imagine if HE had thrown in the towel when he was criticized!

In 1923 Winston Churchill, who had endured some stunning defeats earlier, was defeated in an election and was, for the first time in twenty-two years, out of Parliament. This shocked him into speechlessness. "He thought," noted an observer, "his world had come to an end." In attempting a comeback, he was defeated two more times. By the early 1930s his career seemed finished. He was approaching the age of sixty and was all but washed up and forgotten.

His big unreached goal still stood out in front of him:

the long-shot goal of becoming Prime Minister. Here was a person who defined success as "the ability to go from one failure to another with no loss of enthusiasm." And it was this enthusiastic person who, more than anyone, is responsible for saving the world from annihilation by the Nazi's. It was his personal experience dealing with his own darkest hour that allowed him to lead the World during its darkest hour.

And what carried him from one failure to the next "with no loss of enthusiasm" was his unbridled desire to be Prime Minister. It drove him to "Forget it – Drive On," and that made him stick in the game long enough that when his country called in time of crisis, Winston answered the call.

You must take responsibility for where you are in your life, even if you're not where you would like to be. You must stop looking outside of yourself for why you aren't living the life you think you should be living. If outside circumstances were to blame, no one would ever succeed. Numerous people have overcome outside circumstances in order to escape hard times or difficult situations. It's not those unfavorable situations—it's you!

We stop ourselves time and time again from changing! We think limiting thoughts and engage in self-defeating behaviors. We use indefensible logic to defend these thoughts and habits. We tend to use excuses for everything.

Luckily, there is some good news. You created your circumstances, which means you can change them! Simply change your responses to the events until you get the results that you want. Gain control over your thoughts, images, feelings, and actions. Make these things in alignment with what you want, and eventually you will have what you want. You have control over three things in your life: your conscious thoughts, what you visualize, and your actions. Everything you experience is determined by those three things.

If you don't like what you're experiencing, change these three things. You can change your habits, who you spend your time with, the books you read, the thoughts you tell yourself. In *As a Man Thinketh*, James Allen wrote, "you are today where your thoughts take you; you will be tomorrow where your thoughts take you." You choose where your thoughts are taking you!

People only complain about things they can control. We don't complain about gravity. We don't complain that we're the third planet from the sun. That means that the vast majority of things we complain about are things that are in our control.

The world doesn't owe you anything; you're the creator of your world! Results don't lie. Pay attention to your results. They will tell you what is or isn't working in your life. The only starting point that works is reality. You are ultimately in charge of whether to listen to or agree with any thought you have. Just because you think it or hear it doesn't mean it's true!

If I had to pick one character trait that I think is a "must have" in order to change our results and be successful in any endeavor, it would be persistence. In fact, it seems to be the one trait that is the dominant trait in every single World-Class Goal Achiever I know. I believe it to be the one trait that any ordinary person can use to become extraordinary ("extra-ordinary").

Jack Canfield believes persistence to be the single most common quality of high achievers. Persistent people simply refuse to give up. The longer you persist, no matter how difficult, the more likely you are to succeed. Sometimes, the Universe will test your commitment to your goals. As Norman Vincent Peale says, "it's always too soon to quit!"

Lack of persistence is a major cause of all failure. Without persistence, it is nearly impossible to achieve success in any field or endeavor. However, persistence CAN be accumulated, for it is merely a state of mind. The amount of persistence one uses towards any goal is directly influenced by the amount of desire one has towards that goal. By building a stronger fire under your desire to achieve, you will naturally increase your level of persistence.

In ***Think and Grow Rich***, Napoleon Hill identified 8 factors of persistence.

The first factor of persistence is **definiteness of purpose**. He says that knowing what one wants is THE MOST important step towards the attainment and development of persistence. One will be able to surmount many difficulties when one has a strong **purpose**.

The second factor of persistence is **desire**. When you have a goal backed by a strong **desire**, it is far easier to remain persistent, versus when you don't have a strong desire to achieve that goal.

The third factor is **self-reliance**. If you believe you can carry out a plan that you have set forth, you are able to encourage yourself to follow through and persist, no matter what obstacles may appear.

The fourth factor of persistence is **definiteness of plans**. No matter how weak or strong your **plans** to carry out your goal may be, any sort of **plan** is good support for remaining persistent.

Hill's fifth factor of persistence is **accurate knowledge**.

Having support, whether experienced or observed, that shows your plans are sound and well-based is far more effective and reliable than just guessing what you should do. If you follow in another's footsteps when achieving your goal, you're more likely to persist than if you do it all on your own.

The sixth factor of persistence is **cooperation**. Sympathy, understanding, and harmonious **cooperation** with those around you is good ground for developing and maintaining persistence.

Willpower is the seventh factor of persistence. Hill defined **willpower** as the habit of concentrating your thoughts towards the plans that will help you achieve your goals. By focusing on your plans, you will automatically be reminding yourself of your goal, and your **definiteness of purpose** (the first factor of persistence).

The eighth factor of persistence is **habit**. Daily habits that are aimed towards your **definiteness of purpose** and **desires** automatically bring about persistence.

Along with these eight factors of persistence, Napoleon Hill also identified the sixteen symptoms of LACK of persistence. These sixteen symptoms must be avoided in order to reach and achieve your goals and dreams.

The 16 Symptoms of Lack of Persistence

1. Failure to recognize and clearly define exactly what one wants
2. Procrastination
3. Lack of interest in acquiring knowledge to help support one's goals
4. Indecision; avoiding issues, instead of facing and dealing with them

5. Not creating and finding solutions to problems

6. Self-satisfaction

7. Indifference; compromising, rather than meeting with oppositions

8. Not taking personal responsibility; blaming others for one's mistakes, and believing unfavorable circumstances to be unavoidable

9. Weakness of desire

10. Willingness and eagerness to quit at the first sign of defeat

11. Lack of organized plans

12. Neglecting to move on ideas or opportunities when they are presented

13. Merely wishing instead of taking action

14. Compromising with poverty; absence of ambition for personal ownership

15. Trying to create shortcuts to success; trying to receive without first giving

16. Fear of criticism; not taking action out of fear of what others will think, do, or say; this fear may reside in the subconscious, and therefore isn't easily recognized

Opinions are the cheapest and most readily available commodities on Earth. If you listen to the opinions of others, and are all too ready to let those opinions influence your beliefs and actions, you will have no true desire of your own. You'll be too afraid of what others may think of your specific desire.

It's your choice completely whether you focus on the eight factors of persistence, or the sixteen symptoms of lack of persistence.

Success comes to those that are success conscious, and failure comes to those who are failure-and-fear conscious. Fear listens to the reasons NOT to persist. Remember, fear is there to keep you safe. If you want to stay safe, by all means, remain where you are. But more than likely, you want to dream big and achieve big! If that's the case (and I bet it is), continually focus on the eight factors of persistence. By doing this simple step, you will have even MORE support to accomplish your goals.

Hill also identified four steps which lead to the habit of persistence.

The Four Steps to Develop Persistence

1. Create a definite purpose, backed by a burning desire that will lead to its ultimate fulfillment.

2. Create a definite plan, and carry that plan out through continuous and enthusiastic action.

3. Close your mind tightly and unerringly against all negative and discouraging influences. This includes negative suggestions given to you by friends, family members, and acquaintances.

4. Build a friendly relationship with people that will continue to support your purpose, and who will help you to follow through in achieving your dreams and goals.

Occasional or rare effort to apply these rules and principles will be of little value to you or anyone else. You must apply these rules until following them has become an automatic and fixed habit.

To help you apply these principles, and remain persistent with your goals, it is important to focus on **POSITIVE** emotions and feelings, rather than negative emotions and feelings. According to Napoleon Hill, there are seven major positive emotions and seven major negative emotions. The emotions you feel are readily and automatically passed on into your subconscious mind. Your subconscious mind is ultimately neutral. It feels and does whatever you tell it to feel and do.

The seven major **POSITIVE** emotions are **desire, faith, love, sex, enthusiasm**, **romance**, and **hope**.

These seven emotions are most beneficial to creating a success-driven life. These emotions can only be mastered through **use**. So use them to your advantage!

The seven major negative emotions, to be avoided at all costs, are fear, jealousy, hatred, revenge, greed, superstition, and anger.

The mind cannot harbor both positive and negative emotions at once. Therefore, immediately form the habit of using and applying the positive emotions. Eventually, they will dominate your mind so much that the negative emotions cannot even enter (unless you let them!).

One of our main weaknesses is the average person's all too familiar relationship with the word "impossible." People are all too aware of the reasons why something will NOT work. They know all of the things that CANNOT be done.

If you have children, you'll recognize one of the key ways to develop persistence. What happens when you have your young child in a store and they spot something they want? Maybe it's a particular candy, cereal or toy. Depending on their age (and their desire for the object of their attention) they can become very animated and loud in demanding that you purchase the object for them.

If your on-spot discipline (or threat of discipline) doesn't get them to shut up—and it won't if they really want the object—the only way to quiet them down is to either remove them from the area of their object or in some other way distract them.

What drove Winston Churchill is the same thing that drives your child. It's the total focus on an object of desire. As long as the object is there, and as long as the desire for it is *consuming, obsessive, pulsating and burning* (remember Secret #2), a person will continue to do whatever it takes to satisfy their desire for the object.

That's a critical lesson when we need to shore up our persistence.

WORLD-CLASS ACHIEVERS ALWAYS FAIL FORWARD

An equally important lesson is the need to learn how to "fail forward" as John Maxwell describes it. World-Class Achievers NEVER see failure as the end of the road. It's simply another step in the progress toward their goal.

Many people would consider bankruptcy as the ultimate failure, and unfortunately many people who go through it never recover because they think it's the end of the road. Here are just a few of the World-Class Achievers who came back from bankruptcy:

J.C. Penney (at age 65)

Henry Ford (Twice!)

Walt Disney

Donald Trump

Samuel Clemens (also known as Mark Twain)

Willie Nelson

Burt Reynolds

Robert Kiyosaki

Mark Victor Hansen

Search engine giant Google's attitude toward failure is no doubt one of the reasons the company dominates its market and is the darling of Wall Street. Here's an excerpt from a Washington Post story:

"Although Google places a premium on success, it appears to shrug off failure. The resulting culture of fearlessness permeates the 24-hour Googleplex, a collection of connected low-rise buildings that looks like a new-age college campus… Google employees are encouraged to propose wild, ambitious ideas often. Supervisors assign small teams to test them.

Philip Remek, an analyst who follows Google for Guzman and Co., sees the many initiatives as a series of lottery cards.

"A lot of them aren't going to work," he said. "Maybe there will be a few that take off spectacularly. And maybe they're smart enough to realize no one is smart enough to tell which lottery card is the winner five years out."

"If you're not failing enough, you're not trying hard enough," said Richard Holden, product management director for Google's AdWords service, in which advertisers bid to place text ads next to search results. "The stigma (for failure) is less because we staff projects leanly and encourage them to just move, move, move. If it doesn't work, move on."

But my favorite (true) story of an example of failing forward is about Maxcy Filer. In 1966 Maxcy took the California Bar exam for the first time at the age of 36 and he failed. He took it again and he failed. He took it again and again and again, and each time he failed. He took it in Los Angeles, San Diego, Riverside, San Francisco and anywhere else it was offered. He took it when his children were still living at home and he took it with each of his sons when they had earned their own law degrees. He took it after he started working as a law clerk in the law offices of his sons, and he kept taking it even as he reached an age when most people are thinking of retirement.

After twenty-five years, $50,000 in exam fees and review courses, and 144 days of his life spent in testing rooms, Maxcy Filer took the bar exam for the 48th time, and he passed. He was 61-years-old. Maxcy never saw each failure as the end of his dream. They were merely another step toward the inevitable dream that he had a burning desire for.

In his book ***Psycho-Cybernetics***, Maxwell Maltz emphasized this point that we are not our failures. He stated that we are not our mistakes, for mistakes can be corrected! A statement you can repeat to yourself is, "I am neither my best nor my worst decision. I am a successful, capable person who makes my share of mistakes, and that's all there is to it."

When you really accept that you are not your mistakes, you are able to acknowledge them, learn from them, place them to the side, and move on from them, without staying stuck and focused on them. Most successes are not achieved in a straightforward line. Rather, they are achieved in a zig-zag manner.

Continually focus on your failures, and you will receive more failures. Accept your failures, but consciously choose to focus on your successes. Focus on the successful attempts you have made. Remember, reinforce, and dwell on the attempts.

Use errors and mistakes as a means of learning, then dismiss them from your mind. Ask any successful person, someone you admire, if they have ever failed. More than likely, they've had more failures than successes! But they CHOSE to focus on their successes. They accepted that failure is a necessary part of the path of the successful. Learn from them, and choose to fail forward!

Your talents, abilities, and powers are readily and always within you. It's your choice whether you focus on what you CAN'T do, or if you focus on what you CAN do.

Which are YOU focusing on? Chances are, what you are resisting most is what you most need to embrace.

NOW IT'S TIME TO TAKE ACTION:

On the next page is part of an exercise from **The TGR Seminar** program which is based on the original version of *Think and Grow Rich*. Take the time to complete it and take your persistence to the World-Class level.

Persistence Test

a. Do you have a clear picture of your burning desire? Yes ☐ No☐

b. Have you written a Statement Of Definite Purpose? Yes ☐ No☐

c. Have you decided what you will give in return for your success? Yes ☐ No☐

d. Have you set a date for accomplishment of your goal? Yes ☐ No☐

e. Have you created a plan to accomplish your goal? Yes ☐ No☐

f. Is that plan written down where it can be added to and modified as needed? Yes ☐ No☐

g. Have you written an Affirmation Statement that tricks your subconscious into thinking you have already attained your burning desire? Yes ☐ No☐

h. Do you read these statements at least twice a day – morning and night? Yes ☐ No☐

i. Have you changed your environment and surrounded yourself with symbols that remind you of your goal and resemble your life once you achieve it? Yes ☐ No☐

If you have any No answers you may be suffering from a lack of persistence and seriously undermining your success. Complete the following exercise:

• • •

Recommit to your goal – your burning desire. Rewrite (or write) your Statement of Definite Purpose below.

_____

_____

_____

_____

• • •

What will you give in return? What has (will) your contribution to your success be?

_____

_____

_____

_____

• • •

Set a date for achievement.

I achieve my burning desire by _____, 2_____.

• • •

Create your plan. What specifically have you done (or are going to do) to achieve your goal?

_____

_____

_____

_____

_____

_____

_____

_____

_____

_____

• • •

Rewrite (or write) your affirmation statement: One paragraph, clear, concise.

_____

_____

_____

_____

_____

_____

Remember to read this statement aloud at least two times each day. Read it right now and then again tonight.

• • •

How have you (or will you) change your environment? Pictures, posters, photos, goals sheets, etc…

_____

_____

_____

_____

_____

_____

_____

_____

_____

_____

_____

_____

• • •

If something in your life doesn't turn out as planned, ask yourself: How did I create that? What were my beliefs and thoughts at the time? What did I not say or not do to cause that result? What should I do differently next time in order to get the desired result?

_____

_____

_____

_____

_____

_____

_____

_____

_____

_____

_____

_____

_____

Secret #10:
Do What Others Won't Do Today
So You Can Do What Others Can't
Do Tomorrow

IT'S THE ENTIRE SUBJECT of the classic book, *The Common Denominator of Success*, by Albert Gray—World-Class Achievers simply do the things that others *will not do* (make sure you understand I didn't say the things that others *cannot do*).

Here's a short passage from the book: "But this common denominator of success is so big, so powerful, and so vitally important to your future and mine that I'm not going to make a speech about it. I'm just going to "lay it on the line" in words of one syllable, so simple that anybody can understand them.

"**The common denominator of success—the secret of success of every person who has ever been successful— lies in the fact that "THEY FORMED THE HABIT OF DO- ING THINGS THAT FAILURES DON'T LIKE TO DO."**

It's just as true as it sounds and it's just as simple as it seems. You can hold it up to the light, you can put it to the acid test, and you can kick it around until it's worn out, but when you are all through with it, it will still be the common denominator of success, whether we like it or not."

Wow! That's pretty direct—and pretty simple to understand!

Most people aching to succeed but always coming up short are of the misguided opinion it's because of some big thing they didn't do or some big shortcoming that they have. The fact is, it's not either of those—more often than not, it's the small things they didn't do. It's tied to their daily habits.

It's important to know where our actions come from. Our actions most directly determine whether we succeed or fail at a goal. Our habits play a big part in whether or not we achieve our goals. How do we acquire our habits in the first place? In Shad Helmstetter's book *What to Say When You Talk to Yourself*, he identifies five steps that control our success or failure.

The first step that controls our success or failure is our **behavior**: what we do or don't do. This step most directly controls your success or failure. If your actions work with you instead of against you, it's more likely for things to work for you. Your actions are what control your successes and failures the most directly. We usually know what's right and what's wrong. The reason that we don't always do what's right is due to something that affects and controls our actions, which is:

2. Our feelings—every action we take or don't take is first filtered through our feelings. Our feelings are physical and physiological reactions to specific thoughts. How we feel about something will always determine or affect what we do and how well we do it. If we feel good or positive about something, we will behave more positively about it. Our feelings directly influence our actions. The feelings you hold about anything you do will affect how you do it. Believe it or not, your feelings are completely controllable! Only YOU control your feelings. No one can make you happy or sad; it's entirely

up to you! Thoughts and feelings go together. Feelings are the soil that our ideas and thoughts grow in.

What causes you to have certain feelings? They are created and controlled by your:

3. Attitudes—the perspectives from which you view life. Whatever attitude we have about something will affect how we feel about it, which will determine how we act about it, and therefore whether or not we will do it well. Our attitudes play an extremely important part in whether or not we become successful. A good attitude is essential for achievement in any field or endeavor.

Everything you do is affected by your attitude, either directly or indirectly. Your attitude about yourself automatically determines the attitudes you have about everything around you. Before you can change your attitude about anything outside of you, you MUST start with the attitude you carry about yourself.

A change in your attitude can affect just about everything in your life. If you want to achieve better results, simply improve your attitude! Having a positive attitude can be THE deciding factor in whether or not you succeed at a goal. Our attitudes directly affect our feelings, and our feelings ultimately affect the actions we choose to take or not take. The right attitude gives us an important boost and can really help us to achieve the things that we want.

If you're not sure what type of attitude you're harboring, simply examine your moods, temperaments, hesitations, and self-talk. Our attitudes make us rich, poor, happy, sad, fulfilled, or incomplete. Our attitude is the single most important factor in every action that we take or don't take.

Look at your attitudes. Examine them. Assess them. Take a mental inventory of your attitudes, both good and bad. Decide for yourself which of these attitudes are helping you, and which are keeping you from living the life that you want to live.

The good news is that you CAN change your attitudes! They're not set in stone. Change your attitudes simply by changing your thoughts. Changing your thoughts will automatically begin to change your attitudes. It's your thinking that counts! Put yourself back in control of your thoughts and of your life. Start talking to yourself the RIGHT way.

Our attitudes didn't just come about by themselves. They are created and influenced by our:

4. Beliefs—what we believe about anything will determine our attitudes about it, create our feelings, direct our actions, and help us to succeed or fail. Our belief towards anything is so powerful that it can make something seem different than it really is. The stronger the belief, the more you'll accept other similar things that support those beliefs. Belief only requires us to think that something is true. It doesn't actually have to be true! That means that reality is based upon what we have come to believe. Each of us has a completely different view of reality.

If we believe we are less than what we consider the best, that is FACT, that is REALITY, to us! That's just the way it is, we say! Luckily, that isn't true at all. It's just true to the person that BELIEVES it's true!

Where did our beliefs come from? Our beliefs are created and directed entirely by our:

5. Programming—we believe what we have been programmed to believe. Our very own conditioning has created

and nearly permanently cemented most of what we believe about ourselves and our world. The result of our programming is what we believe, whether or not it's true.

As you can see, our programming creates our beliefs. Our beliefs create our attitudes. Our attitudes create our feelings. Our feelings determine our actions. Our actions create our results.

All of our habits, whether considered positive or negative, are the result of our previous conditioning. They're a result of the things we learned to do, the things we practiced until they became our natural way to behave and live.

Of course, they're not natural at all (even if they sure seem to be!). We weren't born with any of our habits. Any and all of our negative habits can be replaced with new, positive habits.

Some common negative habits are losing things, disorganization, lying, making excuses, sleeping late, gossiping, blaming others, wasting time, not finishing something we've started, the list goes on and on. Which ones do you identify with? What are some other habits you'd like to replace with more positive ones?

Your current habits are producing your current level of results. If you want to create higher levels of results, you are going to have to replace some of your less productive habits with more productive and effective habits. Your habits affect and determine your outcomes. High achievers don't get to the top by accident or fluke. Getting to where you want requires focused action, personal discipline, and energy, EVERY DAY, in order to make things happen in your life. Your habits ultimately determine and affect your future.

Robert Collier, author of the classic ***The Secret of the***

Ages, wrote that, "Success is the sum of small efforts repeated day in and day out." I have had that quote on my dream board for more than ten years to remind me that my daily routine is more responsible for my success than anything else I do. Give me a list of your daily habits and activities and I can fairly accurately determine your success without any other information.

Before he self-destructed because of some bad off-the-course habits, people watched in awe as Tiger Woods hit golf shots that seemed to defy the laws of physics, but they had no idea how many days that Tiger hit 1,000 or more golf balls in order to become that good.

Our habits and our self-image tend to go together. Change one, and you automatically change the other. The word "habit" once meant a piece of clothing. This is fitting, because we literally wear our habits. They're a part of us. Yet we can change them at will. We have conscious control over our habits. Our habits tend to fit us well. They are consistent with our personalities and our self-images. When we change our self-image, our habits change. Our former habits no longer fit our new self-image. The opposite is also true. When we change our habits, our current self-image no longer fits.

Most of our habits are automatic and require little thought or preparation. Practice something enough, and it becomes effortless. Have you ever practiced something so much that you no longer had to think about it? For instance, riding a bicycle, playing a musical instrument, or learning a new dance step. The reaction becomes automatic and unconscious. Our thoughts, feelings, and emotions often work in the same way. They tend to become habit. We tend to react to similar situations in a similar way.

These habits can be changed, altered, or reversed. All you have to do is make a conscious decision to change them! You will have to practice the new habits and ways of thinking fairly often, until they become a part of you, until they become a new habit. The new habit eventually will replace the old habit, IF you allow it time to do so! You cannot expect change to happen immediately. You're working with decades of previous programming! It takes a MINIMUM of twenty-one days (and usually longer) to form enough new thought connections to REALLY change the way you think, believe, and act.

In his book *The Success Principles*, Jack Canfield identifies two action steps for changing your habits. The first step is to make a list of all of the habits that are keeping you unproductive or are negatively impacting your future. Once you've identified your negative habits, the second step in the process of changing your negative habits is to choose a better, more productive success habit. Develop systems that will help to support your new habits. Put up visual signs and reminders to help you stay on track. Successful people adhere to the "no exceptions" rule. They stick to their productive habits, no matter what!

It's physically impossible to break a bad or unwanted habit. When you're attempting to create a new habit, thoughts connected to your unwanted habit will begin to arise. Harness your conscious brain's power at this precise moment! Think a new thought, ANY new thought, not related to your bad habit. In time, the pathway containing the bad habit thoughts will atrophy.

You must allow a minimum of, you guessed it, twenty-one

days, for the bad habit thoughts to cease firing. Be consistent and persistent. Change your thoughts, and you change your habits. Take control of your thoughts and habits, and you automatically take control of your life!

Our physical actions are the outward expression of our inner thoughts. You can't do more than you believe you are capable of. You can't perform winning habits if you don't think you are a winner. Our actions, our habits, will not change unless and until we take conscious control over them. The good news is that this is more than possible; it CAN be done!

The reason we admire greatness is because consciously or unconsciously we recognize that it's achieved by ordinary people who gave a little extra (extra-ordinary).

You possess the key to your own ignition switch! Create the habit of generating enthusiasm in whatever you do. Take the advice of Ralph Waldo Emerson: "Enthusiasm is one of the most powerful engines of success. When you do a thing, do it with all your might. Put your whole soul into it. Stamp it with your own personality. Be active, be energetic, be enthusiastic and faithful, and you will accomplish your object. Nothing great was ever achieved without enthusiasm."

When you express passion and enthusiasm, you become a magnet to others. People are attracted to high levels of energy. They will want to support you in achieving your goals and dreams. Use the power of enthusiasm to help you get what you want.

One of the most powerful habits high achievers use for gaining control over their actions, and ultimately over their lives, is to plan their day the night before. This is a VERY powerful strategy for increasing your productivity and success. When you go to sleep, your subconscious mind will work to help you achieve these tasks upon awakening. It will think of creative ways to overcome obstacles and solve problems. It will send out thought waves that will help to attract to you the people and resources you need in order for you to accomplish your tasks and goals.

When you already know what you want to accomplish for the day, you can start your day off in a positive and focused way. You know exactly what to do, and in what order. Practice the "Rule of 5" everyday: do five specific things that will move your goals towards completion. Decide on those five things the night before, and you will REALLY move towards your goals quickly and effectively.

Becoming more organized is an essential habit to adopt in order to be successful at anything you do.

- Take some extra time to organize your work area on a regular basis.
- Keep up with paperwork by taking care of it yourself or by having someone else do it for you.
- Use file folders, desk organizers, and labeled storage boxes to help keep your paperwork organized.
- Prioritize your projects.
- Make deadlines for yourself, and stick to them.
- Keep an appointment and planning book with you every day.
- Use a portable voice recorder to help you remember ideas throughout the day.
- Break down overwhelming tasks into smaller tasks.

These simple ideas will make a huge positive difference in your level of organization.

I've been blessed to meet some very special people in my life but I've never met anyone who was extraordinary. In getting to know them it's evident that they are just ordinary people who simply *did* something extraordinary. And it always was a result of the things they did that most others would not do.

I'll never forget what Denis Waitley told me about one of his habits. While most people were watching some meaningless show during prime-time television, Denis was writing. Every single one of his best-selling books was written while others were being entertained.

Denis didn't do anything that millions of other people couldn't have also done. He simply did what others would not. It's not any more complicated or difficult than that.

Most successful people have gotten into the habit of writing down a daily task list. The book **Think Like a Winner!** has an effective idea for identifying items placed on your daily "to do" list. Write out your daily "to do" list the night before. List all of the major tasks you need to complete for that day. Prioritize them using the letters A, B, and C. "A" items are those that must be done right away, "B" items are important, but don't require immediate attention, and "C" items require little or no action, but are items of general interest.

To formulate items on your "A" list, follow the "Pareto Principle." This principle is named after the Italian economist and sociologist Vilfredo Pareto. This important and well-known principle holds that 80% of a day's value is contained in merely 20% of the day's actions and tasks. You may complete only the first two items on a list of ten items to complete that day. However, completing just those two tasks will allow you to reap 80% of the list's total value.

By sticking to your "A" list, you will be off to a running start, and will avoid the temptation to focus on and complete the less desirable or effective tasks. You must avoid the lower value items that make up 80% of your list, and instead concentrate on the few high value items that need your immediate attention. By doing this step, you will significantly increase your effectiveness everyday.

Did you know that there are some very simple habits that, if performed on a daily basis, can quickly and dramatically increase your brain's level of performance?

One such habit is sitting up straight. Sit up straight for smarts! Your brain needs 30 TIMES more blood than any other organ in your body. When your spine and shoulders are hunched over, blood flow is immediately limited to your brain. The journey of the neurotransmitters to its receptors is impeded. They can't complete the necessary journey because they don't have enough oxygen to finish the job.

This process is similar to having a kink in a garden hose. A simple snag in the hose stops or severely slows the process of water passing through the hose. When you are hunched over, the amount of energy sent to your brain is reduced. Your thinking ability will be reduced, and you won't even consciously be aware of it! Poor posture can even lead to mini strokes. The lack of oxygen flow to the brain causes tiny blood vessels in the brain to burst. The brain cells supplied by that blood will cease to function, and a stroke soon follows. So sit up straight for smarts!

Another great habit to establish that will do both your brain and your body good is the habit of drinking ample amounts of water. When messages travel from brain cell to brain cell, they have to cross a gap known as the synaptic gap. This gap is filled with water, and this gap is where neurotransmitters are released. Neurons move through that fluid in order to connect to other neurons.

If you're even 5% dehydrated, scientists estimate that 1/3 of those neurons don't successfully connect to other neurons. That's a lot of lost messages! If you're 10% dehydrated, as much as 50% of the neurons don't complete their signals!

Your ability to solve problems and resolve issues is dramatically reduced, and you and those around you suffer the consequences. Making decisions and resolving conflicts are necessary steps in becoming a goal achiever and winner in life. Dehydration causes you to have limited access to your brain's memory storage areas.

How much water is enough to drink for one day? Unfortunately, the answer to this question is not simple. Different scientists have different views on this issue. The statement "drink eight glasses of water a day" is NOT scientifically based. However, if you wait to drink water until you're thirsty, you're already dehydrated! By that time, the messages your brain sends, telling you you're thirsty, are already delayed, and you've been suffering from dehydration for longer than you even consciously knew.

So, bottom line, make sure you drink water constantly throughout the day. Keep a convenient water bottle on your desk to remind you to drink it, and be constantly sipping it. Drink water, and you will be that much more likely to be a goal achiever.

Another habit to adopt along the goal-achieving path

is very simple, and yet very effective. Scientific studies have proven that exposure to light is as effective in combating a depressive mood as are antidepressants! Sunlight is the most powerful. So get out of the office and go for a short walk. Sit out on the balcony or deck and drink your coffee.

Another habit you can do is a habit that will strengthen your corpus callosum, the tissue that connects your left brain and right brain. By continually doing activities that utilize both sides of your brain simultaneously, you will be better able to make decisions, and those decisions will be well-rounded.

Here is the activity: sit down in a chair, and take your right foot and raise it in the air. Make it go in a clockwise circle. At the same time, take your right index finger, and make a six in the air. This exercise forces you to think with both sides of the brain at once.

Another exercise seems goofy while doing it, but it is really effective and stimulates both sides of your brain at once. Take your right index finger and touch your nose. Take your left hand and cross it underneath your right hand. Grab your right ear with your left index finger and thumb. Feel silly? Sometimes the silliest activities are the most effective.

Another habit is a fun one that really makes a positive impression to your conscious and subconscious brain. Just laugh! Laugh and have fun, even if you have to fake it. You may not believe the laugh consciously, but remember, your subconscious brain takes everything you say, do, and think as literal. Positive chemicals and neurotransmitters will be released. The statement "laughter is the best medicine" IS scientifically proven! Don't wait, start laughing now!

Over and over we hear about the importance of physical

exercise. Of course we know that physical exercise is important for our body. But did you also know that exercise is like food for our brain? It is! Exercise in ANY form is brain food, and it naturally reduces stress. Exercise naturally and automatically helps us to release negative energy.

Scientists have proven that just thirty minutes a day, performed six days a week, helps to increase our thinking skills. If you vary the exercises you perform, the development of new brain connections is enhanced, and the flow of neurotransmitters is increased. Your brain performs better, even if you were previously a couch potato.

Crossword puzzles and even sex also stimulate your brain in a similar way. They're mental exercises. The physical act of running has been shown to even slow the aging process! Running 30 minutes, four days a week, builds up a bank of brain cells within the brain. If brain cells degenerate in the future, these brain cells can be replaced by the cells held in your "brain bank."

There are even more benefits to physical exercise! Exercise releases endorphins and helps to create an overall sense of well-being. Blood flow to the brain is increased, which nourishes the brain and promotes optimal functioning. Exercise actually gives you more energy and helps to keep you from feeling lethargic. Your metabolism is increased, and your appetite is kept in control more easily. Physical exercise helps to create a more balanced level of melatonin production, and your sleep cycle is enhanced.

So exercise not only for your health but also for your brainpower and overall optimal level of performance!

Another simple daily habit we can acquire for aiding in

the learning and achieving process is an adage we have all heard during our lives: "an apple a day keeps the doctor away." Turns out, there really IS scientific merit in this statement!

A study done at Cornell University found that apples help to fight brain cell damage and help to prevent Alzheimer's. They also help to flush toxins out of our body by binding to the toxin. The apple acts like a glue to the toxin and the toxin is released through the body, along with the apple. So listen to what your mother always told you, and eat an apple a day! Your body will thank you for it.

We've all heard it before, "take your daily vitamins!" Doug Bench puts a new twist on this statement by offering the following daily vitamins:

1. Whenever someone asks you how you are doing, you MUST ALWAYS answer with a positive statement, no matter how you are feeling! Remember, 5/6 of your brain takes this statement as true.

2. Commit to accepting total and full responsibility for your results and how you feel, everyday.

3. Learn something new everyday. The more you learn, the more information will be at your disposal when future problems and conflicts arise.

4. Recognize and stop every negative statement you say out loud or silent. IMMEDIATELY turn that statement into a positive.

5. Do something not like you everyday. Do something strange, unusual, and different everyday. Doing so will help to create more brain connections and expand your comfort zone.

6. Set a goal by writing it down. The simple act of writing helps to build stronger and longer lasting brain cell connections.

7. Willingly and eagerly fail at something every single day. You will activate your Amygdala and expand your comfort zone.

8. Everyday, tell at least two people you love them, and one of these people must be yourself. You will release positive neurotransmitters both in your brain and in the receiver's brain.

9. Everyday perform an exercise regimen for your body, your mind, or preferably both. You will automatically strengthen your brainpower.

10. Stop and see what everyone else is doing, and do the opposite! Most people are NOT goal achievers or focused on success. See what everyone is doing and do the opposite!

11. Stand up and scream, "I am fantastic, and I can achieve anything! I have tremendous brainpower!" You'll soon believe it.

NOW IT'S TIME TO TAKE ACTION:

Start with the habit that's more responsible for the success of World-Class Achievers than any other habit: the habit of reading. As my friend, Charlie "Tremendous" Jones, says, "you are the same today as you'll be in five years except for two things: the people you meet and the books you read."

Exercise 1: Start with a list of the classic books like *As A Man Thinketh*, *Think and Grow Rich*, *The Magic of Thinking Big*, *How to Win Friends and Influence People,* and others. Spend at least 15 minutes reading every evening just before retiring. This is when your alpha wave level is at the highest in your brain and your subconscious is most impressionable. It's the same principle that happens when you watch a scary movie just before bedtime and then have bad dreams. Only now your subconscious is going to be spending the night working on the outstanding wisdom of James Allen, Napoleon Hill and other giants.

• • •

Exercise 2: Another daily habit to adopt is what Jack Canfield refers to as "the evening review." Each night, before going to sleep, ask yourself the following questions:

Show me where I could have been more effective today.

Show me where I could have been more conscious today.

Show me where I could have been a better _____ today. (i.e. mother, father, doctor, friend, etc)

Show me where I could have been more loving today.

Show me where I could have been more assertive today.

A number of events will come to mind in response to these questions. Observe them without any judgment or self-criticism. Keep asking until no more events come to mind.

Take each incident that arises in your mind and replay it the way you would have preferred it to happen. Recreating this event in a more beneficial and helpful way will help you to act this way during a similar future event.

This exercise will help you to be more accountable for your actions and to determine what better actions to take tomorrow and the rest of the days to come. It will make a huge difference in your life if you commit to it on a daily basis.

• • •

Exercise 3: In order to acquire something new or achieve a new goal, we must make room for it, both physically and psychologically. When we don't throw away items we no longer need, or clear time in our schedules to begin something new, we're unconsciously telling ourselves that we don't trust our abilities. We need to complete our past in order to create a new present.

The following is a list of things to complete before moving forward, taken from *The Success Principles*:

Former business activities

Promises not kept, acknowledged, or negotiated

Unpaid debts or financial commitments

Closets overflowing with clothes never worn

A crowded and disorganized garage

Unbalanced check books and overflowing desk drawers

An attic or basement filled with unused items

A car filled with trash and clutter

Pictures never put into an album
People you need to forgive

The list goes on and on. To help you embrace any change, ask yourself the following questions:

What's changing in my life that I'm currently resisting?
Why am I resisting that change?
What am I afraid of in regards to this change?
What am I afraid might happen to me as a result of this change?
What would I need to do in order to cooperate with this change?
What's the next step I could take in order to cooperate with this change?
When will I actively take this change?

Form the habit of regularly asking these questions. Your answers will change each time you ask them.

NAPOLEON HILL, WHO INTRODUCED millions to the idea of the Master Mind, wrote that, "No two minds ever come together without, thereby, creating a third, invisible, intangible force which may be likened to a third mind."

Formally, or informally, World-Class Achievers understand and employ the power of the Master Mind.

Simply speaking, a Master Mind is anytime two or more people come together (with today's technology it need not be in person) with a common purpose and the intent to benefit from the resulting synergy.

Hill defined the Master Mind as "coordination of knowledge and effort, in a spirit of harmony between two or more people, for the attainment of a definite purpose."

Formal Master Mind groups may be established for a specific purpose, like a group focused on Masterminding marketing ideas. It may be industry specific or topic specific. Members of our Champions Club get involved in a Master Mind group for a year with other members for the specific purpose of helping one another achieve their goals.

There is synergy of energy, commitment, and excitement that participants bring to a Master Mind Group. The beauty of Master Mind Groups is that participants raise the bar by challenging each other to create and implement goals, brainstorm ideas, and support each other. Master Mind participants act as catalysts for growth, devil's advocates and supportive colleagues. It is the ultimate accountability tool.

Science has proven that the simple act of talking releases positive hormones in the brain. Talking is a form of thinking. Talking about an issue or problem in a Master Mind group helps you to feel good, and helps those in your group to generate positive feelings as well.

The human mind is a form of energy. It is spiritual in nature. When the minds of two or more people are coordinated in a harmonious nature, an indescribable and invisible force is created. Two or more brains, in a spirit of harmony and friendship, will provide significantly more thought energy than a single brain.

This phenomenon is similar to plugging in a group of electric batteries. The collected energy of a group of batteries is significantly higher than the power of one battery alone. The increased energy created through a group of like-minded individuals becomes available to every person in that group. It's not limited to a mere few; rather, its power can be harnessed by anyone involved in the Master Mind process.

The tycoon Andrew Carnegie had a Master Mind group of fifty individuals with whom he surrounded himself. The purpose of his Master Mind group was to manufacture and market steel. He attributed his entire fortune to the power he accumulated through his Master Mind. The process is yet unknown, but significant economic advantages may be created and acquired by anyone who surrounds him or herself with a group of like-minded people. These people are more than willing to lend aid and advice to their group. Everyone benefits in the process.

Conrad Toner of Peterborough, Ontario has been a member of Champions Club for two years. He questioned whether he should renew for the second year because he didn't think he could top what he did in his first year (he quit his job, started a business and tripled his income).

But in the second year he's done even better. He has a soon to be released book and a weekly segment on his local TV station. These accomplishments are just the beginning of another outstanding year. Here's what he said about his Master Mind experience: "The ideas, motivation, sounding board and occasional reality check that came from my master mind group was the greatest benefit for me."

Not only does Conrad benefit from the synergy of the Master Mind but also by participating he's also doing what all World-Class Achievers do—they associate with "like-minded people." You're probably never going to be a millionaire if all you ever hang out with are thousand-aires. And it's not likely you'll ever see a billion if you're content to hang out with millionaires.

When Napoleon Hill described the Master Mind Alliance concept in *Think and Grow Rich*, he was writing about something he learned from the tycoon Andrew Carnegie. Carnegie told Hill that his multi-million dollar fortune (he'd be a multi-billionaire in today's dollars) was the result of the 50-person Master Mind Alliance that he participated in. Now that's one powerful Master Mind!

The easiest way to tell if the people around you are worth listening to and following is very simple: listen to their self-speak. What do they say when they talk about you, themselves, or anything for that matter? Winners speak in a way that produces winning and successful results. Winners don't necessarily have perfect or great days everyday. That's pretty near impossible! They just choose to focus on the positives, rather than on the negatives.

In his audio program "Mind Your Brain Success System," Doug Bench praises the importance and rewards of being involved in a Master Mind group. He suggests forming a group with 2-5 other people, preferably with people that are at or above your level of achievement. They should be people that have already accomplished things you want to accomplish. When someone in your group praises you, neurotransmitters called endorphins are released automatically. Your pleasure impulses are increased, and your body's pain receptors are inhibited. When you are around like-minded people, you naturally feel good!

Your Master Mind team will help you to remain accountable and responsible for your thoughts, beliefs, and actions. George Washington Carver said that "99% of all failures come from people who have a habit of making excuses." Your Master Mind team will help you to become aware of limiting thoughts and excuses you may not have even known you were creating! They want you to succeed, and will help you to get from where you are to where you want to be.

Along with the support of the Master Mind you have another friend close by. Imagine how wonderful it would be if we had someone supporting us every step of the way, someone we could count on every day. They would be our closest and dearest friend.

Believe it or not, we DO have that friend. They've been with us our whole lives! That friend is inside of us, within us. They've always been there. We've just been ignoring them. Our friend is there for us, whenever we need them. Use the principles you've learned thus far to help you get to know this inner friend.

This friend is sleeping within us. It is a sleeping giant, waiting to be awakened. It needs the motivation that comes from within us. If we feed and nurture it, everyday, it will help us to conquer our fears, slay unforeseen obstacles, and lead us onward towards our goals. It is a magical genie waiting to be released. It has been waiting a very long time for our guidance. It is a self-fulfilling and essential part of each of us.

Professor Elmer Gates of the Smithsonian Institution was a recognized genius and a world-renowned inventor. He made a daily habit of invoking his subconscious and calling up creative ideas and pleasant memories. He strongly believed that this daily practice helped him in his daily endeavors immensely. He said that if a person wants to improve, "let him summon those finer feelings of benevolence and usefulness, which are called up only now and then. Let him make this a regular exercise, and at the end of the month he will find the change in himself surprising. The alteration will be apparent in his actions and thoughts. Morally speaking, the man will be a great improvement of his former self."

So utilize the support of a Master Mind AND of your inner resources. Using the two together is a magic combination that will propel you towards success and achievement.

NOW IT'S TIME TO TAKE ACTION:

Seek out a local or virtual Master Mind group that you can participate in. (If you'd like a virtual group, check and see if we have openings in our Champions Club.) Make a commitment to attend all of the meetings and to give more to the group than you take.

Secret #12:
It's about Principles

IF YOU'VE READ THIS FAR, you've probably read some new information but you may not have found any new secrets. In other words, you've probably heard all this from someone else before, but hopefully we've given you some new ways to look at it that you can relate to.

So now that you've made it this far, I'm going to reward you by telling you the real secret of World-Class Achievers. Are you ready? The real secret is—there is no secret. That's right! <u>All World-Class Achievers know that there are no secrets, there are only PRINCIPLES</u>.

Stop and think about it. How could so many successful people keep it all secret? That thought never occurred to me as I was desperately seeking to learn the "secrets" that I knew must exist. The day that it finally dawned on me that there really weren't any secrets was an exciting day of revelation.

So why didn't I call this report "13 Principles" instead of "13 Secrets?" Because it would probably have only been read by 10% or less of those who chose to read it because they thought they'd learn something that few others know.

The bottom line is that our Universe (and everything in it) is governed by a set of laws (principles). If your life is in harmony with those principles then, by design, you are an open receptacle for all of the abundance of the Universe.

You've no doubt heard of the principles like the law of

cause and effect (Brian Tracy calls this the most important principle in the universe), the law of attraction (this was the focus of the worldwide blockbuster DVD *The Secret*), the law of reciprocity, the law of compensation, etc.

World-Class Achievers respect principles and they live their lives by them. Are they human, do they struggle? Sure. As I've already written, they're ordinary people and they have to deal with the same temptations and same challenges that all humans do. The difference is, they always go back to the principles.

Legendary NFL coach Vince Lombardi was such a big believer that winning football games was all about basic principles that its said he would begin every season by holding up a ball in front of his team as he said, "Gentlemen, this is a football."

NOW IT'S TIME TO TAKE ACTION:

Take the most negative circumstance that exists in your life today and apply the law of cause and effect to determine what the real cause of the circumstance was. Then create a plan that will address and change the cause.

Secret #13: Seek Out World Class Mentors and Coaches

AT ONE TIME AMBITIOUS U.S. parents would pack their kids in the car, use all of their sick time and vacation time, take most of their life savings and drive across the country to a ranch outside Houston, Texas. Their destination was a training camp run by arguably the best gymnastics coach in history, Bela Karolyi. He produced nine Olympic champions, fifteen world champions, sixteen European medalists and six U.S. national champions. Having your child coached by him increased their chance of future success by an astronomical amount.

World-Class Achievers have always known that secret: if you want to maximize your potential in anything, hire a coach. Coaching is to performance what leadership is to an organization.

A personal coach supports you in a positive way. They give you praise and encouragement. These positive statements automatically and subconsciously release neurotransmitters, endorphins, and hormones. These chemicals give you a feeling of pleasure. Having a positive, uplifting, and inspiring coach will definitely increase your achievement levels!

Alex Rodriguez, or A-Rod as he is affectionately known to baseball fans, is only the highest paid player in the major leagues ($275 million contract). Behind that accomplishment no doubt is A-Rod's life coach who emails him a daily affirmation and has called him before every game for a number of years.

And just in case you're thinking, "Oh, if I earned $32 million a year I'd have a coach too," A-Rod hired his coach long before he became the highest paid player.

Mentors are another "must have" by all World-Class Achievers. Going back to Secret #5, achievers know the importance of "standing on the shoulders of giants."

Here's a very tiny list of World-Class Mentors and their Mentees:

- Richard Burton mentor to Sir Anthony Hopkins
- Audrey Hepburn mentor to Elizabeth Taylor
- Johnny Carson mentor to Jay Leno
- Joe Weider mentor to Arnold Schwarzenegger
- James Dean mentor to Dennis Hopper
- Theodore Roosevelt (26th US President) mentor to William Taft (27th US President)
- Franklin Roosevelt (32nd US President) mentor to Lyndon Johnson (36th US President)
- Margaret Thatcher (British PM) mentor to John Major (British PM)
- Bing Crosby mentor to Frank Sinatra
- Mariah Carey mentor to Christina Aguilera
- Woody Guthrie mentor to Bob Dylan
- Patsy Cline mentor to Loretta Lynn
- Freddie Laker mentor to Richard Branson
- Earl Shoaff mentor to Jim Rohn
- Jim Rohn mentor to Tony Robbins

Now here's some that get real exciting to me:
- Andrew Carnegie mentor to Napoleon Hill
- Napoleon Hill mentor to Earl Nightingale
- Earl Nightingale mentor to Bob Proctor
- **And Bob Proctor is one of MY mentors!**

Nothing has influenced my success more in the last decade than what I've learned from Bob. And I come away from every interaction with him with another powerful insight that blows down yet another one of my self-imposed barriers.

Doug Evans, a CPA from Michigan, is someone I've had the great pleasure to mentor. Doug says, "Vic, through the Champions Club provides you with thoughts, inspiration, motivation and direction to improve any aspect of your life. I now feel I have better focus and a solid foundation for succeeding as I move forward."

Carnegie had his own mentors. But if you just begin with him you find the chain of wisdom that he imparted has made its way over the generations and landed in Michigan, where I know it will be further imparted to those that Doug mentors.

You don't necessarily have to have a person-to-person relationship to receive the benefits of mentoring. One of my personal heroes (and mentors), Winston Churchill, is obviously not available for a person-to-person relationship. But I have learned a lot from him (his writings) and about him (other people's writings) and have studied him intently.

Technology today has made it possible to have person-to-person mentoring relationships all over the world by telecoaching, email, IM and webinars. There is no excuse not to have coaches and mentors on your team.

Jack Canfield describes in his book ***The Success Principles*** the importance of having a coach or mentor. A coach will help you:

- **Clarify your vision and goals**
- **Support you through your fears**
- **Help you remain focused on your goal**
- **Determine specific action steps to take to help you achieve your goals**
- **Determine your values, vision, mission, purpose, and goals**
- **Recognize opportunities**
- **Achieve balance in your life while accomplishing your business and career goals**

There are business coaches, marketing coaches, writing coaches, and personal coaches, among many others.

Even better, BECOME a personal coach or mentor! All of us have a skill we excel at and feel good at while performing. Not only does receiving positive feedback help you feel good, GIVING positive feedback and encouragement releases positive chemicals in both your brain AND the person that is receiving it. Not only will you be helping yourself, you will be helping those around you to reach higher levels of success and achievement.

NOW IT'S TIME TO TAKE ACTION:

Make a decision today that you will seek out some mentors and coaches to work with. Write the decision down, put a date for accomplishment on it and sign it. Review the commitment at least twice a day until completed. If you really want to secure your commitment, fax it to me at 877-233-1557.

Chapter 14
Skyrocket Your Results

So there you have 13 Secrets of World-Class Achievers. I'm betting that there were at least a few of them that were new to you—or at least presented in a way you'd never seen before.

Now the big question is—what are you going to do with them?

If you've gone to the trouble to print them out, I can assure you they will never be worth more than the paper they're printed on unless you start right this minute to do something to act on them (remember Secret #7).

And I can further assure you that if you will put them into practice they will become priceless beyond the wealth of Solomon (or even Bill Gates), in your lifetime. Because although you may never achieve their wealth, the richness of the life you will live will be beyond your wildest imagination.

You already have all of the needed tools. You were born with everything that you need to achieve what you have always wanted, to live the life you have always imagined. You can change just a little, and gain a whole lot.

When you first read these pages of self-belief and goal achieving, they can appear to be not much more than words on a page, sitting there idly. BRING THEM TO LIFE! Begin to practice the exercises and tools that have been brought before you. Make them your own. Make them a part of you.

It's up to you.

Are you ready to start now to live that life?

The principles and techniques I have presented in this book always work. You simply have to put them to work for you! Simply decide upon what you want, believe you deserve it, and practice the techniques and exercises placed in this book. They ALWAYS work!

"It's time to start living the life you've imagined." This statement was spoken by Henry James. This is truly a statement to live by.

Remember I shared part of a letter from John West earlier? Here's the complete letter that I received from him:

"For SO many years I set goals, only to see them remain incomplete and transferred from one year to the next. Sometimes I might actually see a goal achieved, maybe two, but there was never any structure to these successes and there was little hope the succeeding year would be any different. The Champions Club has changed all that and made this year one of the most powerful and empowering of my life.

I had five major goals for the year and multiple secondary goals. Two of the major goals have been achieved, albeit slightly different than envisioned, and the other three are very close to culmination. About six of the secondary goals were accomplished and even more are moving forward. This has never happened before and with 60 days to go, I am daily making momentum-increasing advancement, powered by consistent action.

The accountability factor on a weekly basis with my Mastermind group has been invaluable and the vital link in my chain of successes. The daily habits developed, the book of the month, the seemingly endless resources offered, along with Vic's real caring for each of us and strong unwavering leadership, all have contributed to a life changing experience that I will forever benefit from."

John West

Beverly Hills, CA

www.JDoubleU.com

These secrets worked for John just as they will work for you. Remember this important point: "The Universe is no respecter of persons. It only respects principles." If you apply these principles you'll get the same results as John and every other World-Class Achiever.

I hope you had a pen in hand the entire time you read this book. I hope you were completing the exercises and diving right in.

If not, then please go back and do just that! **This isn't the end—this is the beginning!**

And this is a matter of life and death. Bob Proctor once said, "We come this way but once. We can either tiptoe through life and hope we get to death without being badly bruised, or we can live a full, complete life achieving our goals and realizing our wildest dreams."

That's the choice you're being presented with today. You can either tiptoe through life—or you can change your life.

As we says in the Champions Club: "You're a Champion! You Can Do This!"

Now go do it!

• • •

Get a FREE Smart Goals Worksheet and Video
http://www.Get-Smart-Goals.com

Free copy of the classic *As A Man Thinketh*
www.AsAManThinketh.net

For the Champions Club and other great resources
www.TheChampionsClub.org

About The Author

ELEVEN YEARS AGO Vic Johnson was totally unknown in the personal development field. Since that time he's created six of the most popular personal development sites on the Internet. One of them, AsAManthinketh.net has given away over 400,000 copies of James Allen's classic book. Three of them are listed in the top 5% of websites in the world (English language).

This success has come despite the fact that he and his family were evicted from their home sixteen years ago and the next year his last automobile was repossessed. His story of redemption and victory has inspired thousands around the world as he has taught the powerful principles that created incredible wealth in his life and many others.

Today he serves more than 300,000 subscribers from virtually every country in the world. He's become an internationally known expert in goal achieving and hosted his own TV show, Goals 2 Go, on TSTN. His book, *13 Secrets of World Class Achievers,* is the number one goal setting book at both the Kindle store and Apple iBookstore. Another best seller, *Day by Day with James Allen,* has sold more than 75,000 copies and has been translated into Japanese, Czech, Slovak and Farsi. His three-day weekend seminar event, Claim Your Power Now, has attracted such icons as Bob Proctor, Jim Rohn, Denis Waitley and many others.

His websites include:
AsAManThinketh.net
Goals2Go.com
MyDailyInsights.com
VicJohnson.com
mp3Motivators.com
ClaimYourPowerNow.com
GettingRichWitheBooks.com
LaurenzanaPress.com

Made in the USA
Columbia, SC
29 May 2019